Dearly Bought, Deeply Treasured

THE UNIVERSITY OF SOUTHERN MISSISSIPPI

1912-1987

Detail, original design for campus by the architect R. H. Hunt

By Chester M. Morgan

Dearly Bought, Deeply Treasured

THE UNIVERSITY OF SOUTHERN MISSISSIPPI
1912-1987

THE UNIVERSITY PRESS OF MISSISSIPPI
JACKSON AND LONDON

This volume is sponsored by THE UNIVERSITY OF SOUTH-
ERN MISSISSIPPI

The paper in this book meets the guidelines for perma-
nence and durability of the Committee on Production on
Guidelines for Book Longevity on the Council on Library Resources.

Photography Credits

Mississippi Department of Archives and History:
    p. viii (Eudora Welty Collection)
    p. 8, Henry L. Whitfield
    pp. 36–37, 1923 view of campus

Hattiesburg American:
    p. 128, campus riot of 1967
    pp. 168–69, NIT photographs

Bob Hand Photography
    p. 162, aerial photograph of Jackson Memorial Stadium

Library of Congress Cataloging-in-Publication Data

Morgan, Chester M.
    Dearly bought, deeply treasured.

    Includes index.
    1. University of Southern Mississippi—History
I. Title
LD3425.M67   1987   378.762'18   87-22999
ISBN 0-87805-307-7 (alk. paper)

British Cataloguing in Publication available

Contents

Preface

This volume began as a pictorial history to be accompanied by an edited collection of essays on various aspects of the university's history. As the project unfolded, it was decided that a single narrative text would provide a thematic unity that neither the photographs nor separate essays could achieve. When I assumed the task of writing such a text, I became the beneficiary of the labors of a great deal of other people. The completed history owes much to the extraordinary efforts of the authors of those original essays: Ed Polk Douglas, Stanley R. Hauer, William D. McCain, Clarice Wansley, Pauline Stout, and C. J. "Pete" Taylor; and to the editorial work of Frank N. Walker.

The bulk of the photographs included in the book were found in the University of Southern Mississippi archives housed at the William D. McCain Library and Archives on campus. The limited number of actual prints and negatives in the university's archival collection left significant gaps, however, which could only be filled by reproducing photographs from additional sources. Most of those came from school yearbooks and campus newspapers, though a few came from various other individuals and institutions. Unless otherwise noted on the copyright page, therefore, the pictures included were acquired from university sources.

With almost no personal experience or expertise in photography and with very limited visual sensibilities, I chose the photographs for the volume with a great deal of trepidation. In some sense, the selection process was the most difficult aspect of my task. Many people or events which perhaps ought to have been included in the illustrations were not, because of space limitations or because such photographs were of poor quality or did not exist at all. In making the selections, I received valuable counsel from many people, especially Dick Ford, David Bodenhamer, JoAnne Prichard of the University Press of Mississippi, and my wife, Mary Jane Morgan. Their advice enhanced the book immeasurably, though whatever deficiencies remain should be attributed not to them but to me alone, since I made the final decisions.

In the course of producing the book, I have become indebted to many people: to President Aubrey K. Lucas and Seventy-Fifth Anniversary Committee Chairman Peggy Prenshaw for their confidence; to Warren K. Dunn, P. W. Underwood, Ben Willoughby, William D. McCain, Nell McCall, William B. Taylor, the Mississippi Department of Archives and History, the *Hattiesburg American*, and the staffs of USM's Office of Sports Information, Public Relations Office, and McCain Library and Archives for access to photographs; to USM Photo Services and Broadcasting Services for reproduction of photographs; to John Gonzales and Polly Stout for their insight and tactful correction of errors; to Sandra Boyd for her valuable proofreading; to Lena Sizemore for her excellent typing; to the staff of USM's Oral History Program for their indulgence; to JoAnne Prichard of the University Press of Mississippi for her patience and competence; and to my family for their perseverance. I owe a special debt of gratitude to Terry Latour and Cathy Gaskin, who facilitated my access to the university archives; Michael Seal, who tirelessly reproduced hundreds of photographs; Dick Ford, who contributed his labor and his remarkable artistry in countless ways; and most of all to David Bodenhamer, whose confidence, patience, and encouragement sustained me from start to finish.

Introduction

Dawn broke damp and cold that day, as Orville Brim recalled it almost half a century later. Though the campus, still pockmarked with pine stumps, was shrouded in mist, he could make out on that crude excuse for a road that ran in front of the college, an unhurried little band, trudging their mysterious way through the morning, like figures from those yet unwritten Faulkner novels. In his mind he could still see them—despite the intervening years—almost as clearly as he had seen them then: the three men walked beside the ox-drawn wagon upon whose unsided floor huddled two women and two children around a fire insulated from the wagon bed by a mound of earth and embanked all around with brick and stone. He remembered wondering who they were and where they might be going. "What satisfactions and disappointments did the day hold for these simple country folk? When would they reach home, tired and cold? What was home like? What were their days and years like? What were their dreams?"

The occasion of Brim's reminiscence was the golden anniversary of Mississippi Normal College, which had that very year, 1962, become the University of Southern Mississippi. He had served on the first faculty in 1912, and of all the memories that might have forced their way into his consciousness as he reflected on the institution's early years, this scene was perhaps the most fitting. "The children on that wagon," he concluded, "through the widening influence of the college and its teacher product, must have experienced a richer life than the parents ever knew." Indeed, placing a richer life within the grasp of such "simple country folk" as these was the vision that gave birth to what is now the University of Southern Mississippi.

Today it is a thriving comprehensive university, the largest in Mississippi, striving to give its students, in the words of its current president, "the knowledge and understanding they will need to live creatively and joyfully, as well as . . . the skills they should have to establish a satisfying career." In its quest for academic distinction, however, the university remains committed to its original vision. In the midst of the seventy-fifth anniversary celebration, of which this volume is a part, President Aubrey K. Lucas reaffirmed that commitment. "Our goal," he said, "must be to develop the human capital" of Mississippi. "Our history gives us confidence that we . . . can contribute in significant ways to our state's social and economic progress. And it is in this way that we can become a truly distinguished university."

It is a noble heritage, born of adversity and nurtured through three quarters of a century of struggle. Mississippi was a poor state in 1912, but there were some, like Joseph Anderson Cook and Thomas P. Scott, who were determined that it should not remain so. They—and hundreds like them among Mississippi's public school teachers—believed that education offered the state its best hope for overcoming poverty. It was their conviction and their determination that gave birth to Mississippi Normal College.

But neither birth nor growth came easily. "In all probability," said Alma Hickman, who taught with Orville Brim on that first faculty, "the hardest battle ever fought, or ever to be fought, by the institution was an economic one. How does a new school, born in a depressed area during bad times, secure the necessary students and funds to become solvent?" Looking back, Brim thought he saw the answer in the character of the school's first students. "We are all familiar with the oft quoted statement, 'Easy come, easy go,'" he wrote in 1962. "One can see this demonstrated on every hand in this age of abundance." There is, however, another principle, "equally true but little recognized," Brim argued, that best captures the spirit of "the students who came in the early years to Mississippi Normal College." That principle is, "dearly bought, deeply treasured." For rural families like those described in the opening paragraphs of this introduction, the school was a godsend. Before 1912 children of such families could look toward higher education only with hopelessness, and even the normal college, inexpensive as it was, demanded "saving, personal and family sacrifice" from students who hoped to attend. Those who made it "paid a hard price," said Brim, "but they valued this opportunity. . . . They were so in earnest, so eager . . . so appreciative . . . so thankfully responsive . . . that it was touching . . . I only wish," he later lamented, "that while at Hattiesburg I had known as clearly as I do now the background from which the students came and the spirit that lived within them. The situation has grown clearer through the years. I was young and inexperienced. I gave honestly and earnestly, but I wish I might have shown more appreciation for the effort they were making and more admiration for their courage."

Teachers like Orville Brim and the students he described laid for the institution a firm foundation, one that has endured now for seventy-five years. During that time, others—students, faculty, and friends—have given honestly and earnestly, transforming that small normal college for the training of rural school teachers into one of the South's major state universities. Today the University of Southern Mississippi continues its pursuit of excellence. As the university and its friends look forward with confidence to completing a century of educational achievement, it is fitting to cast a backward glance at its heritage. What follows is not a comprehensive history, but rather an effort to capture faithfully, in photographs and brief narrative, the spirit of that heritage—one "dearly bought, deeply treasured."

Mississippi Normal College

1910 - 1924

"The Normal College," said the school's first yearbook, "stands for clean, pure, efficient lives." But for many Mississippians at the dawn of the twentieth century, life was anything but clean, pure, and efficient. More often it was like that of the eighteen-year-old boy whom rural school principal T. P. Scott described as "reared in . . . ignorance, inured to hard . . . labor, and hemmed in by provincialism in its narrowest form." The youngster's long dormant ambition suddenly took life, however, when "he found himself possessed of an opportunity to attend school." Convinced that many other rural children shared this one's "intense earnestness and determination to secure an education," Scott devoted himself to finding some way to allow such earnestness and determination to bear fruit.

Though most Mississippians by 1900 endorsed the principle of public education, the state's public schools still faced enormous practical problems. More than eighty percent of all school-age children were in rural areas where they depended on country schools, whose terms ran six months at best and often no more than four. Three-fourths of these were one-room schools in which the frustrations of presiding over all grades drove teachers to

a transience rivaling that of the sharecropper families from whence so many of their pupils sprang. More than six teachers in every ten moved annually, while the average tenure at any one school was barely a year and a half. Another twenty percent each year were teaching school for the first time anywhere. These harried but devoted educators were the driving force that created Mississippi Normal College.

Before 1912 teacher training was at the mercy of scattered summer normal institutes lasting one to four weeks and offering little more than review courses in preparation for the state examination for teaching licenses. From the day of its founding in 1877, the Mississippi Teachers Association (MTA) worked tirelessly for the establishment of a state normal college. Finally, in 1906, a normal college bill was introduced into the legislature, only to die in the hostile House Education Committee. The following year, MTA President Joe Cook devoted his entire 1907 annual address to the issue, sounding a note that would fundamentally alter the tactics of the normal school forces and ultimately lead to success. The lawmakers had rejected pleas for a normal college, Cook suggested, because they did not believe its advocates were "speaking for five

thousand teachers and three hundred thousand children. Let us help make the Legislature believe," he urged. "Let us five thousand teachers speak for ourselves and ask the fathers of more than three hundred thousand white children to speak for them!"

Thus began a campaign of organized publicity and personal contact that would eventually overwhelm the opposition in what the *Jackson Daily News* called "one of the great legislative fights of the decade." After a second normal college bill died in committee in 1908, State Superintendent of Education J. N. Powers turned to T. P. Scott, then head of the Brookhaven city schools, to organize a campaign in support of a third bill, which Representative Marshall McCullough intended to introduce in 1910. Scott had served the MTA since 1901 as secretary, vice-president, and president. During those ten years he had cranked out an endless stream of mimeographed letters to county superintendents of education and newspaper editors throughout the state urging their support for the teachers' association as well as for the general interests of education in Mississippi. The Brookhaven superintendent now trained the sights of his little hand-operated mimeograph machine

3

Representative Marshall McCullough of Lincoln County, right, sponsored legislation that created Mississippi Normal College in 1910. The driving force behind the bill was the Mississippi Teachers Association whose monthly publication, far right, was a forceful advocate of public education in the state.

upon the enemies of McCullough's House Bill 204, who soon found themselves besieged with letters, telephone calls, telegrams, and editorials from all parts of Mississippi urging establishment of the normal college. Gradually Scott's self-proclaimed "propaganda methods" took their toll. With the aid of a strongly worded special message of support from Governor Edmund F. Noel, and after supporters reluctantly allowed opponents to strike the appropriation clause, the bill passed the House on March 16. A week later the Senate approved it, and on March 30, 1910, Governor Noel signed it into law.

It was an act, as T. P. Scott put it, which seemed to its enemies "worth less than the paper on which it was written." Stripped of any appropriation, the bill granted no more than "the bare right" to build a college. Two other bills, however, approved on the last day of the 1910 session, at least offered supporters a possibility of turning "right" into reality. They allowed counties and municipalities to issue bonds to finance land, buildings, or other inducements to aid in "procuring the establishment and location of the Mississippi Normal College." Governor Noel appointed the institution's board of trustees, which met for the first time on

May 7, 1910, in the governor's office. They decided to solicit bids from cities interested in securing the school but agreed to accept no donation short of $100,000 plus a building site. Three communities made offers: Jackson and Hinds County, $200,000 and a sixty-acre site; Laurel and Jones County, $230,000 and a sixty-acre site; Hattiesburg and Forrest County, $250,000 and a 120-acre site. Several other cities, including Meridian and Artesia, eventually showed some interest, but by September attention focused on the two piney woods towns, Laurel and Hattiesburg. The board visited Hattiesburg on September 6, Laurel the next day, and then met on the 16th to select the location. The vote was Hattiesburg – six, Laurel – two, Jackson – one.

Hattiesburg in 1910 was Mississippi's fastest growing city and had been so for a decade. In less than thirty years, it had blossomed from a sleepy way station on Captain William H. Hardy's New Orleans and Northeastern Railroad into a bustling New South city. The early wooden buildings clustered on a few mud streets surrounding the railroad depot had given way to imposing brick office buildings and elegant dwellings along paved streets that sprawled out over an area large enough

Mississippi's harried teachers often presided over as many as eight grades simultaneously in one-room schools like Jackson County's old Roberts School, which now stands in the courtyard of the Education and Psychology building on the USM campus.

HATTIESBURG, MISS.

THE LOGICAL POINT

FOR THE

STATE NORMAL SCHOOL

SEPTEMBER SIXTH
1910

HOTEL HATTIESBURG

MENU

Lake Shrimp Cocktail

Queen Soup   Pin Olas

Baked Snapper, Egg Sauce
Pommes Sautern

Loin of Beef Financiere.
French String Beans

Squab Chicken on Toast, French Peas in Cases

Asparagus Vinaigrette

Ice Cream   Fancy Assorted Cakes

Imported Swiss Cheese
Sunshine Sticks

French Coffee

Community leaders organized a campaign, left, to persuade the MNC Board to locate the new college in Hattiesburg, which in the first decade of the twentieth century was a bustling New South city, below.

to be crisscrossed with eight miles of street railways. The agent of the transformation was an economic boom that, as historian John Ray Skates put it, "rode on railroads and was fueled by lumber." Hattiesburg was the capital of the South's yellow pine industry and the hub of four major railroads over which moved six million board feet of lumber a day to New Orleans, Mobile, Jackson, Meridian, Natchez, and beyond them to the nation and the world. Almost everything in the town served the mills and railroads in one way or another: supply houses, machine works, shops, roundhouses, hotels, wholesale grocers, and countless jobbers. Hattiesburg boasted the state's wealthiest bank, largest lumber mill, largest electrical generating plant, fourth largest population (almost 12,000), and now the state's new normal college.

Throughout the fall of 1910, the city and the college board wrestled with the problem of a location for the school. W. S. F. Tatum, a local lumber baron, offered three possibilities, including the campus of old South Mississippi College, which W. I. Thames had founded in Hattiesburg in 1906 and whose main building had burned to the ground earlier in the year. Tatum's most serious challenge came from Dr. T. E. Ross, A. A. Mon-

In 1912 the elegant President's Home, left (now the Alumni house), and the girls dormitory, Hattiesburg Hall, opposite page, stood in stark contrast to their desolate surroundings.

tague, and H. A. Camp, whose so-called Hardy Street site encompassed 120 acres about two and a half miles west of downtown. On December 27, after three months of sometimes heated controversy, the board voted five to four to accept the proposal of the Ross group. The trustees purchased an additional eighty acres—at one hundred dollars an acre—from the same three men who promptly donated the $8000 back to the school. Tatum later gave his South Mississippi College property to the state's Baptists for a denominational school. Mississippi Woman's College, now William Carey College, began its life the same month, September 1912, that Mississippi Normal College opened its doors across town, and the two institutions have prospered together over the last seventy-five years.

In addition to the site, the normal college received several additional considerations from the city and others: extension of both Hardy Street and a parallel streetcar line to the campus; access to the city's gas, sewage, and electrical lines; construction of a railroad spur to the campus by the Mississippi Central Railroad to facilitate movement of building materials; and donation of an additional 640 acres of land to the school by the J. J. Newman Lumber Company.

While a special committee of the board toured several campuses around the country to study buildings, grounds, and other physical aspects of comparable institutions, the George Engineering Company of Memphis conducted a topographical survey of the Hardy Street site. To prepare designs for the campus and its first buildings, the board selected R. H. Hunt of Chattanooga, one of the most prominent and productive architects in the South. He had already designed numerous structures in Mississippi, including buildings on almost every college campus in the state and at least four in Hattiesburg itself.

Hunt conceived his plan for the campus around two major axes, one extending northward from the streetcar station on Hardy Street to the opposite end of the site, the other running east and west and intersecting the first at the location of the present Administration Building. Here was the focal point of Hunt's scheme. Though he did not design the existing edifice, its columned porticoes and imposing dome quite faithfully reflect his conception of the structure that should occupy this crucial spot. Well in front of it was a large shady grove, bordered by a semicircular roadway that branched from Hardy Street at the southeast cor-

ner of the campus and curved gently toward the rotunda and back out again to rejoin the street at the southwest corner. Along this avenue stood four large academic buildings (of which only two, College Hall and what is now Southern Hall, were ever constructed), overlooking the grove and giving the institution, as architectural historian Ed Polk Douglas put it, "a gracious, ordered 'public front.'"

Behind the dome was to be a gazebo in the center of a long, shaded quadrangle extending along the north-south axis to a second semicircle of buildings that anchored the back end of the campus. Three pairs of dormitories faced each other (as Forrest County and Hattiesburg Halls still do) across the quad, men on the west and women on the east.

East of this center campus, Hunt envisioned an almost self-contained secondary complex of buildings for faculty housing. At the south end stood the impressive president's home (now the Alumni House) behind which extended a row of tennis courts and gardens, flanked on either side by seven pairs of buildings. Scattered about the periphery of the campus were smaller auxiliary structures and staff dwellings.

On July 25, 1911, the board approved Hunt's general design and his plans for the first buildings. They included five colonial-style structures of red brick with stone trim: College Hall, the principal academic building, containing classrooms and administrative offices on its first floor, a library and classrooms on the second, and an auditorium and four small rooms on the third; Hattiesburg Hall (in honor of the city's contribution to the college), a three-story dormitory for women; an identical dormitory for men, Forrest County Hall (in honor of the county's gift); a two-story president's home; and an Industrial Cottage for women students. The board received bids in late August and awarded a contract to I. C. Garber of Jackson for $178,591 to construct all five buildings. Work began in October.

Meanwhile the board encountered some difficulty in securing a president for the college. At the December 27, 1910, meeting at which they had approved the Hardy Street location, the trustees settled on Henry Whitfield, president of Mississippi Industrial Institute and College in Columbus (now Mississippi University for Women). After considering the offer for a month, however, Whitfield decided to remain at II&C.

The board then chose W. H. Smith, the state supervisor of rural schools, who accepted in February 1911, and agreed to supervise preparations for the school's opening on a part-time basis without salary until assuming the full duties of the presidency in February 1912. After eight months of trying to launch a new institution, however, he, too, decided to forego the challenge and remain as rural school supervisor. Finally the board turned to Joseph Anderson Cook, superintendent of schools in Columbus, who accepted the job in October 1911, at a salary of $3500 a year. He would remain almost seventeen years.

Though Whitfield and Smith ultimately rejected the presidency of the college, both had been forceful advocates of its creation and held definite notions about what the school should be and do. Their ideas, along with those of Cook and his hand-picked vice-president, T. P. Scott, molded the early character of Mississippi Normal College. That character drew its basic elements from two sources that were common to the background of all four men: educational experience and progressive convictions. All of them had begun their careers as public school teachers and had been stalwarts in the fight for public education in Mississippi. Whit-

The Board first offered the presidency to Henry L. Whitfield, below, who declined and remained head of the Industrial Institute and College in Columbus. He was elected governor of Mississippi in 1923. W. H. "Corn Club" Smith, left, served as president on a part-time basis in 1911. Joseph Anderson Cook, right, was president of MNC, 1911–1928, and Thomas P. Scott, far right, was vice-president, 1911–1930.

field and Smith served as state superintendents of education, Cook and Scott as presidents of the MTA. All but Scott eventually became college presidents: Cook at Mississippi Normal College, 1912–1928; Whitfield at II&C, 1907–1920; and Smith at Mississippi Agricultural and Mechanical College (now Mississippi State University), 1916–1920. A decade after turning down the presidency of Mississippi Normal, Whitfield became governor of Mississippi. Smith personally organized the state's first consolidated school and as state superintendent supervised the establishment of three hundred more around the state. He was best known, however, as a champion of industrial clubs—tomato clubs for girls and corn clubs for boys—that taught practical skills to rural students. Heralded as the father of Mississippi's consolidated schools, he became more universally known as "Corn Club" Smith, a title which he bore proudly.

The first decade of the twentieth century witnessed the high tide of American progressivism, and nowhere did progressive currents run deeper than in education. The concept of teacher training that began to take shape at the hands of Whitfield, Smith, Cook, and Scott clearly reflected those currents. Public education, they agreed, should be practical, professional, and democratic, and they designed Mississippi Normal College accordingly.

Whitfield believed that the existing public schools were deficient because they were "not properly related to life." Traditional curricula focused on training the mind alone, "to the exclusion of those subjects which have a direct bearing on the future lives of the children." The common schools, he suggested, should rather take "children with their native endowments and their pre-school experiences and . . . grow them into men and women who can perform completely the functions of life in a Christian civilization." The work of the normal school, he concluded, was to equip teachers with "the vision, training, energy, and self-sacrificing spirit" for such work.

Smith concurred, suggesting that such subjects as geography, history, and arithmetic should "be taught as the processes by which the business . . . of life [is] carried on and not as isolated, dead studies." He insisted that only professionally trained teachers could accomplish this task. "Let pedagogy and psychology put on their everyday clothes," he said, "and go to work in earnest on the everyday problems of life among the great common people of Mississippi."

No one was more committed to the common people than Joe Cook. His enthusiasm for the democratic way of life permeated every aspect of his thinking, sometimes with ambiguous consequences. Befitting the tradition of Thomas Jefferson, who as the nation's president sometimes greeted visitors in house slippers, Cook "practiced an informality that at times," according to Orville Brim, "verged on crudeness." To him social amenities smacked of aristrocracy and "had no place in democratic living." He even disdained academic credentials, once claiming that the only "D" he ever wanted after his name was "RFD."

As his second-in-command and chief academic confidant, Cook chose one who shared these democratic sensibilities. For T. P. Scott, the principal goal of education was to train not leaders but citizens. He saw the public high school as a kind of "finishing school for the masses," which would "offer a common-sense, practical and efficient preparation for the duties and responsibilities of the life that our boys and girls will of necessity enter upon when they leave." Educators should make students "bold and courageous to grapple with the problems that confront them . . . able not only to pull their own weight, but to 'lend a hand'

to the burden of the other fellow." Scott thought this concept required a fundamental change in the traditional course of study, one that would not lower the standard of academic achievement but "raise it . . . breathe life into it, and clothe its dry bones with flesh." Education, he insisted, should "articulate with Life instead of with musty college walls." The early curriculum of Mississippi Normal College was largely the work of Vice-president Scott, and he infused it with these progressive ideals.

The law establishing the institution had defined its purpose clearly: "to qualify teachers for the public schools." The college bulletin set the minimum age at fifteen but recommended that students be several years older than that before entering. The only academic prerequisite was "satisfactory evidence of having completed the common school course," that is, the eighth grade. A stiffer requirement would have excluded one of the college's principal constituencies, the practicing teachers of the state, many of whom could and did pass the state licensing examination with no more than an elementary school education. The early curriculum, therefore, included a considerable amount of high school work as well as college level courses,

and experienced teachers and high school graduates often found themselves in classes with young common school graduates. This serious defect could only be corrected as the college itself turned out enough trained teachers to supply the state's needs and allow the institution to raise its entrance requirement. Normal students could receive credit for work beyond the elementary level either by presenting a certificate from "an affiliated high school" (without a formal accreditation system, colleges compiled a list of schools whose work was considered acceptable) or "an approved college," or by passing an examination covering the work done.

In accordance with its enabling legislation, the college offered two courses of instruction: a two-year certificate program that qualified the graduate for a teaching license good for five years, and a four-year diploma program leading to a lifetime professional license. Courses were measured in hours, forty for the certificate and eighty for the diploma. Five forty-five-minute recitations per week for six six-week terms constituted one hour. There was an additional six-week summer term that offered both regular course work and review courses in common school subjects for

At right, practice school students, many of them barefoot, eat lunch. Below, science professor R. J. Slay demonstrates a farm waterworks to his class. The announcement of the opening of the college is from the Mississippi Educational Advance.

THE
Mississippi Normal College

HATTIESBURG, MISS.

This is our **State** College for the training of teachers. The first session will begin about September the 15th, 1912.

An excellent faculty is being selected, and the most suitable courses of instruction and training are being prepared.

There is no doubt that this College is facing greater possibilities than any other educational institution in the South.

The buildings are beautiful, convenient, permanent, fire-proof, germ-proof and water-proof.

The laboratories, work-rooms and demonstration plats will be thoroughly in accord with modern educational ideas.

The location is high, dry and free from disease conditions.

For detailed information, write

PRESIDENT JOE COOK,
Hattiesburg, Miss.

(Editorial.)

teachers wishing to prepare for regular state and county teaching examinations.

Scott chaired the faculty committee that governed the catalog and the curriculum, and his influence was evident in both, right down to descriptions of particular courses. The 1913-14 bulletin announced that all classes should emphasize "the correlation of the work of the school with the community life." The Department of English offered courses in reading, grammar, composition, and literature, as well as, of course, the teaching of English. "The work in composition," said the catalogue, "especially in the lower classes, will be connected as closely as possible with everyday life. Themes connected with country life, with its varied needs, advantages, problems, privileges, and opportunities, will be given a large place in both written and oral composition. . . . It is the aim to make all plans of work genuinely democratic." Upper level work covered such courses as advanced grammar, Southern authors, Shakespeare, and nineteenth-century poetry.

Mathematics included arithmetic, algebra, geometry, and trigonometry. History courses—ancient, medieval and modern, English, American, Mississippi, and methods—emphasized, accord-

COOKING BY ELECTRICITY
AN IMPORTANT FUTURE FACTOR

DOMESTIC SCIENCE CLASS, STATE NORMAL SCHOOL
HATTIESBURG, MISS.

Construction was still underway, right, when the school opened in 1912. The original buildings, above, included (from left) College Hall, Forrest County Hall, the Dining Hall, Hattiesburg Hall, the Vice-president's Home, the Industrial Cottage, and the President's Home.

ing to the bulletin, "those movements of the past that seem to be most vitally connected with the present. Everything that cannot be vitalized by something from the life of the student is considered out of date pedagogically. Dates, wars, and politics are considered of secondary importance. Social, economic and industrial movements and problems of the past and present are stressed." Professional education courses were both theoretical—principles of teaching, curriculum, psychology—and practical—observation and practice teaching in the training (later Demonstration) school. Science included botany, zoology, general science, physics, and chemistry. Agriculture, civics, hygiene, geography, manual training for boys and domestic science for girls, drawing, and school music rounded out the required curriculum. Optional work included Latin, French, Spanish, German, and piano.

Officials scheduled opening ceremonies for September 18, 1912, and when the faculty, students, and visitors arrived, what they found was hardly R. H. Hunt's vision of a carefully landscaped neo-Jeffersonian "academical village." Those early students remembered their years in Hattiesburg as "the Stump Age," and with good reason. The cam-

pus had only recently been carved from a vast cut over pine forest, untouched by human hands, as Orville Brim noted,"except to make it more unattractive." The stump-scarred ugliness stretched as far as the eye could see in every direction except east, where the town lay some two and a half miles distant. Rising from this raw terrain, stark and incongruous, stood the five handsome red-brick buildings, accompanied now by several functional wooden structures in various stages of completion, which were designed, according to Ed Polk Douglas, in what "could only be called 'lumber camp vernacular.'" They included a dining hall, a combination post office and college store, a powerhouse, and several dwellings. Excessive rainfall during the year had delayed construction, and evidence of the contractor's continuing presence lay scattered about: piles of dirt and debris, materials and equipment, a half-unloaded boxcar near the front of Forrest County Hall, and the builder's shack to one side, with several workers digging in an open trench to complete the water and heating systems.

The rains, impervious to the mood of anticipation that surrounded the occasion, continued into opening day, adding a sea of mud to the general

unsightliness of the landscape. The steady downpour drenched the crowd but could not dampen the enthusiasm of those who had labored so hard to make this day a reality. By ten o'clock, College Hall's eight-hundred-seat, third floor auditorium was full, the guests including the board of trustees, Lt. Governor Theodore G. Bilbo, State Superintendent of Education J. N. Powers, Rural School Supervisor W. H. Smith, leaders of both houses of the legislature, and assorted local dignitaries. Pastor G. H. Thompson of Court Street Methodist Church invoked the blessing of the Almighty, after which followed the traditional sequence of inaugural oratory: welcoming, thanking, and looking forward to achievement. Joe Cook, presiding, offered special gratitude to the people of Hattiesburg and Forrest County for the land and buildings, adding in an exemplary display of presidential timber, "But, as you see, we need more buildings already." This executive art of yoking thankfulness for past financial favors with urgent pleas for future ones has been refined now through five subsequent presidencies. Lunch followed the opening exercises, after which came a tour of the campus. The next morning all classes met briefly, but instructors spent the bulk of the day classifying students. On

Above, the college barn; top right, entranceway to the President's Home; below right, the Dining Hall. The boardwalk extended from the Dining Hall door to the streetcar station at the front of the campus.

*The first faculty page to appear in the yearbook was in
1915. All but Emily Jones, G. H. Armstrong, A. B.
Dille, C. B. Boland, Jessie May Lomax, and Lorena
Thames were on the original faculty, which also
included R. J. Slay, Annie Faust, and Sadie Chiles who
are not pictured here.*

September 20, regular classes began.

"In the final analysis," Alma Hickman said in her memoir, *Southern As I Saw It*, "education involves students, teachers, and books." The 227 students who attended Mississippi Normal College's first term were, according to history professor Willard F. Bond, "the most sober-faced homesick group of people I have ever seen. Some were crying. Many . . . were farther from home than they had ever been." One got off the train, and spent the whole day in the depot debating whether or not to go back home. "Hunger finally drove him out to the college." Another's father had opposed his going, certain "he would soon be wearing white shirts, collars, and neckties, which . . . would forever ruin him as a farmer." Most rural parents, however, understood the unique opportunity the normal school afforded: an accessible state school, without the social demands or expenses of a traditional university. Despite these advantages, attending Mississippi Normal College still meant great personal and family sacrifice for many, one of whom Brim recalled vividly. His clothes were literally worn to the "point of tatters, sometimes held together by common pins," and the entire family of seven lived in a two-room dogtrot cabin. Yet when

Brim and his wife accepted an invitation to share Sunday dinner in these modest surroundings, they found not only the expected "atmosphere of family love and devotion," but also "an intense yearning for an education for the children." The example was extreme, but the sentiment was typical. A college education was something precious to Mississippi Normal College's early students, and Brim came to admire them greatly.

There were seventeen on the first faculty: Vice-president Scott and Kate Brown (mathematics), J. N. McMillin and Anne H. Augustus (English), W. F. Bond and Alma Hickman (history), W. I. Thames (economics), R. J. Slay (science), Brim (pedagogy),

T. F. Jackson (agriculture), Annie Faust (primary methods), Willa Bolton (geography), May F. Jones (physiology and resident physician), Maggie De Campbell (domestic science), Delora Hanel (manual training and drawing), Lorena Tomson (school music), and Sadie Chiles (observation school). All but four were Mississippians; Brim and Tomson were from Ohio, Dr. Jones from Virginia, and Hanel from Michigan. All but two had earned bachelor's degrees, while Brim, Augustus, and Jackson, in addition to President Cook, held master's degrees. From September 12, until opening day, they met every afternoon in Hattiesburg High School's auditorium to hammer out educational philosophy, curriculum, and guidelines for student classification. New to each other as well as to the institution, they quickly developed an extraordinary camaraderie. Few, if any, had taught college before; several were recent graduates themselves, teaching for the first time anywhere. But they were amazingly dedicated and fell to their task with an infectious enthusiasm. "From the standpoint of terminal degrees they probably did not rank as high . . . as the college professors of today," one of the early students recalled years later, "but they ranked high in 'educated hearts' and 'understand-

At right, the first faculty and student body. The original library, below, was on the second floor of College Hall. President Cook planted chinaberry trees, opposite page, along campus roads to provide both shade and beauty.

ing attitudes.'" For country boys and girls who were earnest yet unsure of themselves, eager but socially unsophisticated, such teachers were a godsend, and the students loved them for it. Brim, who left after three years to pursue a distinguished career that included several years at Ohio State University, declared, "In my many years of college teaching I have never known a staff more sincere in purpose, more selfless in work, more devoted to the welfare and growth of the student body."

As for the third component of Alma Hickman's educational triad, books, the college was not so well endowed. The first library contained approximately five hundred books, a few magazines, and two daily newspapers, housed in two College Hall classrooms and under the care of students. In 1913 the college employed a fulltime librarian, Pearl Travis, but the library appropriation remained less than that of the college farm for several years. By 1924 the library occupied half of the first floor of the newly opened Science Hall and held 6000 volumes, five daily newspapers, and eighty periodicals.

In 1912 the legislature finally appropriated state money for the college, $76,500 to equip and $50,000 to maintain the existing buildings. It

FACULTY AND STUDENT BODY, MISSISSIPPI NORMAL COLLEGE. HATTIESBURG, MISS. JUNE 19, 1913.

proved less than adequate. For four days during the first session, dormitory residents resorted to hauling water in buckets when sand from the campus well clogged the water pump. Had local citizens not come to the rescue, Cook might have been forced to close the school. In an emergency meeting the Hattiesburg Commercial Club raised $7000 to link the campus to the city water supply and then supervised the laying of two and half miles of six-inch cast iron pipe in less than two weeks, a gesture of community support for which the college was profoundly grateful. By the end of the first year of operation, Cook was able to report to the board that initial construction was complete and, thanks largely to student labor, the stumps had been removed and the ground cleared, leaving "the appearance of the institution, while still crude, . . . much more sightly." Prime symbols of the lingering crudeness were the droves of hogs and cows that roamed freely about the campus, bedding down near dormitories where they drew flies, fouled the air, and generally made nuisances of themselves. In the absence of a local stock law, Cook appealed to the board for funds to build a fence, and sometime in 1914 one appeared—supposedly hog-proof with barbed wire and heart

yellow pine posts. For sixteen years it remained, enclosing the entire two hundred-acre campus and, according to Alma Hickman, eliminating the problem of cows. Hogs, if the college newspaper offers any indication, were a different matter. The *Normal College News* reported as late as 1920 that several local swine had become such "an accepted institution" that the campus would have seemed "lonesome without their presence and their cheerful grunts." Nor were they without utility, scavenging "bits of lunch dropped by the town students and the fruit peels that are carelessly thrown down near the store." The editors encouraged students to take more notice of these porcine neighbors and to exercise due care in keeping the campus gate closed lest they wander helplessly outside and meet a swift demise under the wheels of the streetcar. A few years later the *News* again took up the issue, only on a more serious note, urging city officials to help rid the campus completely of animal intruders by imposing a fine on anyone willfully leaving the public gate open.

President Cook labored manfully to beautify the campus. After pushing the grading through to completion in 1916, he planted chinaberry trees along all the roads, oaks in the quadrangle and

elsewhere, a few pecan trees here and there, and Bermuda grass all around. Only the chinaberries flourished, but Cook persevered with the oaks for several years and saw some success. The pecans proved hopeless. Grass did well only where the soil had been well prepared, and for several years visitors found the college's main academic building surrounded by pea patches, which not only enriched the soil but supplemented the dining hall fare. Covered boardwalks connecting the dormitories and major buildings on campus provided some relief from the elements and were replaced in 1922 by concrete sidewalks.

In 1914 the campus got its own post office and a streetcar station—brand new cars running a thirty-minute schedule on school days and every fifteen minutes on weekends. The same year, a second girls' dormitory opened to relieve a severe overcrowding problem. The first campus building financed by state funds, it was appropriately named Mississippi Hall. A laundry (now part of the Industrial Arts and ROTC Building) was constructed in 1918 and equipped with machinery bought from a cleaning establishment in Holly Springs.

Campus life during the early years bore the distinct imprint of two powerful personalities, President Cook and Vice-president Scott. For men with such similar backgrounds and convictions, these two seemed as unlike as any pair could be. Cook was, in Brim's words, "a dynamic, buoyant extrovert," whose pleasant enthusiasm put even "relatively shy students . . . at ease." Almost everyone knew him as "Daddy Joe." No student, however, and few adults dared refer to Mr. Scott by his first name, and some surely wondered if even his own children called him Daddy. The two men's mottoes reflected the irony of their relationship. Cook's "Get there on time and stay to the end"

exuded an optimistic determination that became an almost universal campus slogan. The plaque that hung above Scott's desk also spoke of perseverance, but in a strikingly different tone. "Keep plugging away," it read, "this is not an over-intelligent age."

Colleagues remembered Scott as reserved, cold, austere, and unapproachable. Like Cassius, he "had a lean, hungry look," said Bond. Though many, especially students, feared him, almost everyone respected him. Bond recalled his "rugged honesty" and "devotion to duty," and Brim thought him "a scholar par excellence." Librarian Anna Roberts said that he was "absolutely fearless"

Female students pose at the campus gate, opposite page, and in front of the streetcar, left, which ran from the station at the campus entrance to the corner of Main and Pine Streets downtown.

as a defender of the college, and Emily Jones believed that he, more than anyone else, was responsible for the school's academic progress and ultimate recognition by the national education community. Years later, when they had escaped the bite of his wit and the relentless vigilance of his discipline—which extended even to the sage grass that obscured strategic portions of the favorite hillside courting spot—many students even recalled Scott with some degree of affection.

Cook's most striking trait, other than his abiding sense of democracy, was a frugality that bordered on the penurious. As Alma Hickman said, he watched his own and the school's money "like Silas Marner," and his parsimony permeated every aspect of college life. As a young man he had almost

lost the family's modest plantation through excessive use of credit, and he was determined to instill the virtue of fiscal responsibility in those entrusted to his care. Each edition of the school bulletin contained a section on expenses, listing every conceivable penny a student might have to spend, including the fifty cents a week for laundry and the ten-cent streetcar fare for the round trip to town for worship each Sunday. Other admonitions of thrift were scattered throughout the catalog:

> Each student will be expected to dress with simple and inexpensive taste.
>
> Keep your trunk check until you reach the college. . . . The trunk will be sent for at a nominal expense to you—much less than if you get a drayman yourself.
>
> Do not take a cab or hack to come to the college, as this is a needless expense.
>
> Under no circumstances should bills or silver be sent through the mail in unregistered letters, either to the College Secretary or to students.

Cook counseled parents not to allow their children a great deal of spending money and advised students to deposit surplus cash in the business of-

fice. "Six bits," he insisted, was "enough for a married man to carry around and two bits enough for a single person." The chapel hour, which remained mandatory—with varying degrees of enforcement—until 1955, offered the president a capital opportunity to preach economy to a captive audience, and he made the most of it. "Use all the water you need," he admonished more than one assembly, "but don't let the water run after you use all that is necessary. Keep your bedroom at the required temperature, but don't raise every window as high as you can and try to heat Forrest County."

Cook offered opportunity as well as advice. Any student who desired could defray part of his expenses by working a few hours each day—sweeping, digging stumps, waiting tables, or working the college farm—at fifteen cents an hour. And expenses were not very great: five dollars for the matriculation fee (three dollars for summer term only), four dollars a month tuition (which was waived for students who pledged to teach for a specified period in the state's rural public schools), five to eight dollars a year for books, and approximately seventy-five dollars a year for board (ex-

Above, women's dormitory lobby. The sample board statement, right, from the 1913 Bulletin not only illustrates President Cook's meticulous bookkeeping but also reveals much about wages, prices, and Dining Hall fare.

BOARD STATEMENT.

At the end of each board month (4 weeks) an itemized statement is printed and distributed to the students. The statement for the sixth month of the past session is given below:

To the Students of Mississippi Normal College:—

You will find below a statement of the board account for the sixth scholastic month. The board for the sixth scholastic month is $8.50. This is 20 cents less than last month. I expected an increase instead of a decrease, but the water consumption last month was about what it should have been—40 gallons per day per person. We expect to have only about three weeks more of winter. Continue to co-operate in the management of heat. We are improving in the management of heat. Let us keep on until we learn to manage it scientifically.

The light bill is about as heretofore and the meters do not show any undue amount to any building.

The Cottage girls' board is $5.90—a decrease of 20 cents. They still maintain their good record.

You will note an increase in charge for breakage. This is due to the fact that the charge for breakage heretofore has been found inadequate.

Inspect statement carefully, ask any questions you wish, and send statement home.

Respectfully,
JOE COOK, President.

Statement of Board Account for Sixth Month February 4 to March 3, 1913.

DEBITS

Quantity and articles.	Price	Amount
To amount inventory on hand		$1,387.97
To purchases this month:		

GROCERIES

9 bbls. Flour	$ 5.70	$51.30
1053 lbs. Sugar	4¾c	51.01
100 lbs. Sugar	5¼c	5.25
172 lbs. B. E. Peas	4¾c	8.17
100 lbs. Lima Beans	7¼c	7.25
100 lbs. Bulk Salt	.70	.70
1 bbl. Pocket Salt	3.00	3.00
1 case Condensed Milk	4.00	4.00
6 cases Oatmeal	1.45	8.70
2 cases Macaroni	1.80	3.60
5 lbs. Tea	.35	1.75
62 lbs. Crackers	.07	4.34
4 bu. Meal	.70	2.80
5 38-lb. sacks Meal	.62	3.10
6 doz. Hominy	.75	4.50
1 bbl. Grits	3.50	3.50
50 lbs. Evap. Apples	$ 9½c	$ 4.75
7½ doz. Canned Goods, asstd.	.85	6.38
2½ doz. Canned Grapes	1.00	2.50
2 1-3 doz. Canned Peaches	1.70	3.97
2-3 doz. Preserves	6.00	4.00
1 case Star Naptha Washing Powder	3.85	3.85
132 lbs. Coffee	23½c	31.02
92 lbs. Coffee	.24	22.08
100 lbs. Rice	5½c	5.50
55 gal. Syrup	.45	24.75
1 bbl. Apples	3.00	3.00
1 case Bon Ami	2.50	2.50
1 case Scouring Soap	3.50	3.50
1 bbl. Washing Powder	9.78	9.78
347 lbs. Lard Comp.	0822	28.52
24 lbs. Cheese	1945	4.67
3150 loaves Bread	3 1-3	105.00

(Total, $428.74)

MEATS

Bacon	$ .22	$ 44.54
125 lbs. Bacon Rib Bellies	1387	17.34
1457½ lbs. Fresh Pork	.10	145.75
112 lbs. Fore Quarter Beef	.10	11.20
66 lbs. Hind Quarter Beef	.11	7.26
603 lbs. Hind Quarter Beef	1196	72.12
62 lbs. Sirloin Strips	1445	8.96
108 lbs. Hams	17½c	18.90
182 lbs. Beef Liver	0995	18.11
60 lbs. Pork Sausage	.12	7.20

(Total, $351.38)

MILK AND BUTTER

484 lbs. Butterine	.17	82.28
370 gal. Sweet Milk	.30	105.00
.206 gal. Buttermilk	.15	30.90
74 gal. Separated Milk	.15	11.10
Cream		1.80

(Total, $231.08.)

COAL AND POWER HOUSE SUPPLIES

2 cars Coal		$ 95.89
Freight on 2 cars coal		120.51
53 gal. Cylinder Oil	$ .38	20.14
52 gal. Engine Oil	.23	11.96
54 gal. Coal Oil	.10	5.40
Hauling and unloading coal		69.88
2 Brooms		1.30

(Total, $335.08)

VEGETABLES

100 lbs. Onions	1½c	1.50
2 lots Green Onions		6.00
6 lots Collards		5.03
414 lbs. Turnips	.03	12.42
210 lbs. Cabbage	.02	8.50
10 bu. Irish Potatoes	.85	8.50
31½ bu. Swet Potatoes	.50	15.75

(Total, $53.40.)

EGGS

1 case Eggs	8.00	8.00
71 doz. Eggs	.25	17.75
53 doz. Eggs	.20	10.00

(Total, $36.35.)

Debits—*Continued.*

MISCELLANEOUS

1 ton Ice	6.00	6.00
6 Floor Brushes	1.50	9.00
5 doz. Brooms	3.25	16.25
2 loads Saw Dust	3.00	6.00
Car Fare of Mail Carrier		5.00
Printing adds for bids		12.00
Printing this statement		8.50
Electric Bill		62.19
Medicines		20.25
Laundry of table linen		4.60
Breakage Fund		30.00
Allowance for E. and O.		12.02

LABOR.

Salary of Steward	50.00
Salary of Cook	40.00
Salary of helpers	84.00
Salaries of 25 dining-room girls	150.00
Salaries Bell, Ringer, Mail Carrier, Physician's assistant and sweepers	56.69

(Total, $380.69.)

Total $3,386.50

CREDITS

Inventory of Provisions on Hand as follows:

8 doz. Gelatine at	$1.25	$10.00
13 cans Mince Meat	2.10	2.28
1 case Bon Ami	2.50	2.50
1 case Scouring Soap	3.50	3.50
3 doz. Spices at	.45	1.35
1 doz. Cinnamon at	.85	.85
1 doz. Nutmegs	.40	.40
90 lbs. Cocoa	.30	27.00
80 lbs. Baking Powder at	.28	22.40
10 cans Pie Apples	.85	.71
75 lbs. Coffee	.23 1-2	17.63
1-2 case Matches	4.50	2.25
15 doz. Eggs	.20	3.00
92 lbs. Coffee	.24	22.08
2 1-2 bbls. Flour at	5.70	14.25
1 bbl. Salt at	3.00	3.00
2 doz. Peaches, 3 lbs.	1.70	3.40
6 doz. Pie Peaches	1.00	6.00
6 doz. Pie Apples	.90	5.40
50 lbs. Breakfast Bacon	$ .22	$11.00
60 lbs Ham	.17 1-2	10.50
475 lbs Pork	.10	47.50
2-3 case Star Naptha	3.85	2.58
Part bbl. Light House Cleanser		6.00
Part bbl. Washing Powder		5.00
33 lbs. Evaporated Apples	9 1-2	$3.14
1 doz. Dessert Peaches 10 lbs	8.00	8.00
1 doz. Tomatoes	.85	.85
2 cases Oatmeal	1.45	2.90
20 lbs B. E. Peas	.4 3-4	.95
1-2 bbl. Grits	3.50	1.75
1-2 case Soap	4.00	2.00
1-3 case Soda	3.05	1.02
30 gals Vinegar	.19	5.70
40 lbs. Turnips	. 3	1.20
1 doz. Prunes, 10 lbs.	7.25	7.25
2 doz. Blackberries, 10	8.50	17.00
1 1-2 doz. Corn	.85	1.27
450 lbs. Sugar	. 4 3-4	21.37
1-2 doz. Preserves	6.00	3.00
3 doz. Canned Apples	.85	2.55
4 doz. Brooms	3.25	13.00
650 gal. Syrup	.45	292.50
200 lbs. Lard Comp.	8.22	16.44
45 gal. Cooking Oil	.60	27.00
10 lbs. Bacon Rib Bellies	13.87	1.38
		660.85
Coal on hand estimated		625.00
Total on hand		$1,285.85

Credits From Other Sources:

Good tansferred to Industrial Cottage	61.16
Meal Tickets sold	23.10
Meals to Employees	37.80
Ollie Smith, board	4.32
Lula Hemby, board	.84
Sam Wood, board	$ 9.00
Industrial Cottage for electricity	4.05
Industrial Cottage for heat and water	8.00
Industrial Cottage for Medicine, help, fuel, printing, etc	3.90
Joe Cook, for Ice and Butter	3.18
Joe Cook, for electricity	1.80
Joe Cook, for heat and water	8.00
T. P. Scott, for meals, electricity, heat and water	42.50
College Hall for Heat, water and electricity	40.00
	1,533.50
6104 days Board, ..303* per day	1,853.00
Total	$3,386.50

Statement of Board Account at Industrial Cottage for Month Ending March 3, 1913.

DEBITS

Balance on hand, Feb. 3, 1913	$ 11.78
Goods transferred from dining-hall	61.16
Milk, Eggs and Vegetables	13.75
67 1-2 lbs. Pork	6.75
Laundry	.40
Electric Bill	4.05
Charge for Heat and Water	8.00
Charge for medicine, help and fuel	1.50
Charge for Mail Carrier, Bell Ringer and Printing	2.40
Total	$109.79

CREDITS

Inventory on hand	$ 12.84
Extra meals	2.55
16 Students at $5.90 per month	94.40
Total	$109.79

NOTICE.

Students intending to leave the college during a board month will please note that the Secretary must be advised at the time of such departure; otherwise the board charge will be continued against them. Settlements for fractions of a month will be made on basis of Ten Dollars per month, and must be made at time of withdrawal.

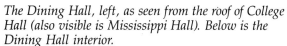

The Dining Hall, left, as seen from the roof of College Hall (also visible is Mississippi Hall). Below is the Dining Hall interior.

cluding laundry). Nonetheless, demand for employment was so great that the school allowed no student more than six dollars a month from student labor.

Discipline at Mississippi Normal College was fairly simple, at least in theory. "Only those of good moral character" would be admitted, and since moral laxity was intolerable in a schoolteacher, any student whose conduct betrayed a lack of self–discipline faced dismissal. "The general rule of the college," concluded the catalogue, "is for each student to do the right thing." The vague simplicity of this dictum reflected both the president's ideals and the student body's general make-up.

Cook encouraged students "by every possible means," said Alma Hickman, "to think for themselves, speak for themselves, control themselves." He attributed his success as an educator to the conviction that most young men and women truly desired maturity, intelligence, and the respect of other people. His system of discipline appealed to those desires. "Put boys and girls on their own responsibility," he said, "and they always respond." Most of the early students, having already taught for several years, were older than typical

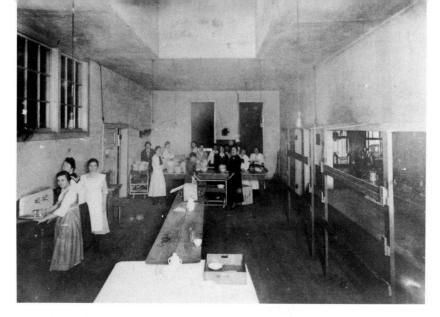

Manual training classes, opposite page, met in the basement of Mississippi Hall until Science Hall opened in 1922. Student workers, left, wash dishes in the Dining Hall. The painted curtain in the chapel auditorium, below, depicts progress from one-room school to modern consolidated facility.

college students and therefore more suited to such an ethic of personal responsibility.

Still, student life was fairly regimented. Each day began with the rising bell at 6:30, followed by breakfast in the 500-seat dining hall. All students dined at the same hour, family style at assigned tables, each of which had a student waitress and a faculty host. A designated faculty member presided at each meal, making announcements and offering thanks for the food. Classes met from 8:30 to 4:00 with chapel at 11:00, where Cook presided over what the bulletin described as "an opportunity to take part in . . . devotional exercises, to hear . . . announcements, and to enjoy many interesting discussions and lectures." The program often included a lecture by some faculty member or a prominent visitor or a presentation by a student organization. Usually Cook lectured or led open discussions on topics ranging from practical campus problems to international issues to philosophical inquiries. He encouraged free and full participation by faculty and students. If flagging interest stifled voluntary contributions, he would often call on students by name, a practice which no doubt contributed to persistent attendance problems. In 1925 after what the campus newspaper

SATURDAY MORNING AT H'BURG HALL

At right, cartoons from the 1920 yearbook. Barely visible behind the couple swinging, opposite page, is the covered boardwalk that connected the Dining Hall to the front of campus. The two buildings in the background are Forrest County Hall, nearest, and Hattiesburg Hall.

SOCIAL HOUR AT THE P.O.

HAS THE MAIL CAME?

SUNDAY AFTERNOON VISITORS

called the annual "wrangle about chapel and chapel attendance," Cook commissioned the faculty psychologist to prepare and distribute a questionnaire on the issue. A faculty-student committee then evaluated the results and made recommendations to the president. There is no evidence that the administration implemented the suggestions or that chapel attendance improved.

The bulletin noted that "proper social intercourse . . . is encouraged." The rules for decorum suggest, however, that Cook either was a strict constructionist on the meaning of "proper" or that he never intended the "encouragement" to be overly vigorous. The only designated social hours were thirty minutes daily between dinner and the 6:30 social hall bell and Sunday afternoons between 2:00 and 5:30. During the weekday periods, couples were restricted to dormitory lobbies, but on Sundays they were allowed to venture out about the campus. Despite persistent rumors that Mr. Scott kept a spyglass on the roof of College Hall, more than one budding romance blossomed atop the partially wooded hill that sat just barely out of sight of the dormitories. A 6:30 p.m. bell sent students to their rooms for study hours, which lasted until 10:15 and were rigidly enforced.

A final bell at 10:30 signaled lights out and the end of the school day.

Students who abused social privileges lost them: kissing could lead to suspension and anything more daring was likely to be a "shipping offense." The rules explicitly forbade smoking, dancing, and for girls under twenty-one, riding in automobiles with men. Cook justified the prohibition of cigarettes, not on moral or health grounds, but because, he said, no school superintendent would hire a man who smoked, an argument the students found less than compelling in light of the president's own inveterate tobacco chewing. By the late twenties the rule became a dead letter, as did the restriction on automobile riding, once people discovered that a car was, in Alma Hickman's words, "a means of transportation" and not a bordello on wheels. The ban on dancing, interestingly, proved the most durable, lasting until the 1940s.

Students could not leave the campus grounds without special permission, and the administration discouraged them from visiting friends in the city or entertaining guests in the dormitories except during specified times. With special permission, students could go into town to shop on Saturdays but had to return to campus for meals. They were

goals of the institution. The YMCA in particular sought to equip men to strengthen and vitalize "the cause of Christ . . . in the rural districts," where graduates, as teachers, would exercise "intellectual leadership." Perhaps more important to the students, however, were the opportunities for fellowship these clubs provided. For simple country boys and girls thrust into an alien social environment, the associations' informal receptions offered a much-needed "means of curing 'the blues.' "

Other social outlets included the four literary societies. The Prestonian and the Platonian offered men a chance "to develop themselves along the lines of oratory, debate and a ready ability to act as leaders in public gatherings and to express opinions when opportunity presents or duty demands." The Sherwood Bonner and the Mississippian involved women in programs of "music, readings, discussions, literary criticism, etc." Again, however, the students were perhaps more thankful for the social opportunities that the societies afforded, such as the Leap Year party that the Sherwood Bonners gave for their brothers the Prestonians in January 1924. Held in the lobby of Hattiesburg Hall, it was a girl-invites-boy affair,

encouraged to attend worship in town on Sunday morning, but, as the *Normal College News* advised, "this does not carry with it permission to visit restaurants, refreshment counters, depots, or any other places except the church."

Religion played a central role in life at Mississippi Normal College. The bulletin urged students to "let no opportunity pass to develop your spiritual nature, since this is even more important than your mental development." And there was no dearth of opportunities: short prayer services each morning in the dormitories, daily chapel devotionals, Wednesday evening prayer services, Sunday morning Bible classes—taught by faculty for credit—Sunday evening campus services, and a

series of revival meetings each session. "These privileges constitute an important factor in college life," said the student newspaper. "If you miss them, you are missing the very best part of the college course."

Among the first student organizations formed on campus were Young Men's and Young Women's Christian Associations, founded to unite Mississippi Normal College's students "in loyalty to Jesus Christ, to lead them to accept Him as their personal Savior, to build them up in the knowledge of Christ, especially through Bible study and Christian service that their character and conduct may be in accord with their belief." Even the work of these associations conformed to the general

Uncle Ned, below, transported students' trunks from the train depot to the campus. His wife Hattie was a favorite with the dormitory girls, who benefited from her sewing, washing, and sage advice, including her oft-quoted philosophy: "Honey, life's just a great big piano, and everybody's playing his own little tune."

highlighted by a proposing game, in which, according to the *Normal College News,* "the genus homo was stood around the room" in a ring while the girls circled them, "proposing to each blushing youth in turn. Some of the proposals [were] fraught with earnestness, and genuine pleading was in the tone of the voices and in the eyes of many of the girls who [pleaded] for a husband." Top prize went to Miss Louise Dawson, whose primary inducement was the possession of a job, which allowed her to offer her candidates the prospect of voluntary and leisurely unemployment. "The vote for her," said the *News,* "was almost unanimous."

There were also tomato clubs for girls and corn clubs for boys, which fostered practical skills and prepared the future educators for their roles as leaders in the industrial movement that so influenced rural education during the era. After 1917, when the Smith-Hughes Act provided federal money for vocational education, the college began to train home economics teachers for public schools. Thereafter, the tomato and corn clubs, along with the egg, poultry, and pig clubs, as well as the cooperative dairy association, were consolidated into a Home Economics Club.

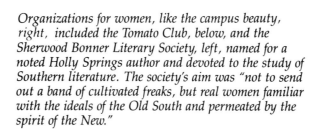

Organizations for women, like the campus beauty, right, included the Tomato Club, below, and the Sherwood Bonner Literary Society, left, named for a noted Holly Springs author and devoted to the study of Southern literature. The society's aim was "not to send out a band of cultivated freaks, but real women familiar with the ideals of the Old South and permeated by the spirit of the New."

Male students studying in Forrest County Hall dormitory room.

Frances Ingram of the Metropolitan Opera Company appeared in concert as part of the college's 1920 Music Artist Series. She poses here, third from left, with campus sponsors of the series.

In 1922 several faculty members, led by Kate Brown of the history department, organized the World Affairs Club. Affiliated with Andrew Carnegie's Institute of International Education, the club was the first of its kind in Mississippi and was limited to forty members selected by the faculty. Lectures at the monthly programs ranged from Hattiesburg businessman "Pep" Jones' address on international trade to Mabel McMillin's discussion of compulsory employment in Bulgaria. A Lyceum series in the early years also brought to the campus Carl Sandburg, Williams Jennings Bryan, and the Cincinnati Symphony.

Early in the 1912 term the students, at President Cook's urging, organized a Student Self-Government Association. All students were members of the association, bound by honor to observe its motto: "Every Man a Gentleman and Every Woman a Lady." Officers included a president, vice-president, secretary-treasurer, and an elected council of eight men and seven women whose duty it was to hear cases of student misconduct and recommend punishment to the faculty. The association, which reflected both Cook's democratic ideals and his belief in individual responsibility, lasted until 1926.

There were also in the early years county clubs, a college quartet, tennis club, debate team, women's glee club, storytellers league, Shakespeare club, and an honor council. By 1925 a school orchestra, commercial club, modern language club, dramatic club, American Legion chapter, and Masonic and Eastern Star orders had been added.

The students published the first yearbook, called *Neka Camon* (an Indian term meaning New Spirit), in 1914. The *Normal College News* first appeared in December 1918, edited by a faculty-student committee chaired by Scott. Published every Saturday during the forty-two week session, the newspaper was primarily a means of exchanging information between the college community and teachers in the field, as well as other supporters around the state.

Cook sent an early edition to Theodore G. Bilbo and solicited the governor's assessment of the modest periodical. "From a psychological standpoint," Bilbo replied, "I am inclined to believe that the *Normal College News* is so small and insignificant looking it might do more harm than good. Why not make it a monthly publication and make

The Dramatic Club of 1922, left.

The 1915 Tennis Club.

it four times as large if you haven't enough money to make the weekly larger? This is a confidential, friendly suggestion." The governor added a more blunt postscript: "The little thing looks puny." In response Cook defended the newspaper's size, listing a host of advantages of a small sheet over a larger one. "Governor," he concluded, in light of his own and Bilbo's modest stature, "it does seem to me that you and I would be the last men in the world to condemn men or things because of lack of corporeal immensity." Bilbo relented, praising the president's valiant "defense of the 'little thing,'" which he noted, "is so compact and complete until I will try to be satisfied with the infinitesimal creature. God bless it in its good work and may no one ever get in its way or step on it, for it cannot stand much. It would be powerless to defend itself against a sure enough attack."

Athletics began modestly at Mississippi Normal College. In September 1912, 150 students organized the Athletic Association and elected Science Professor R. J. Slay as athletic director. At the suggestion of Stella McLaurin of Montrose, the group adopted black and gold as the school colors; they remain so to this day. Football was new to many country boys in 1912, and only after much persua-sion did thirteen "stalwart" souls, two of them one-armed, volunteer for the school's first squad. The inaugural game was a 30–0 thrashing of the Hattiesburg Boy Scouts, coached, ironically, by future State Teachers College President Claude Bennett. Two more wins, a loss, and a tie filled out the opening season. Students walked the mile or so to Kamper Park where home games were played. In its first decade, the school went through five different coaches—Slay, A. B. Dille, B. B. "Opp" O'Mara, Cephus Anderson, and O. V. "Spout" Austin—all of whom coached on a part-time basis. Scheduling proved difficult, and opponents ranged from nearby agricultural high schools, such as Poplarville and Wesson, to Mississippi College, which pounded the "Normalities" on a somewhat regular basis. "They were from a Baptist school," M. M. Roberts later recalled, "but they were mean."

Highlights of the early years included a 113–0 triumph over Mize and a 13–7 near miss against Ole Miss in 1913. Low points were more frequent, including humiliations at the hands of Mississippi College (75–0 in 1916), Southwestern Louisiana College (66–0 in 1923), and the University of Mississippi (54–0 in 1920). Notable players included

Athletics at MNC

One, two, three, four;
Two, four, three, four;
Who in the world are we for?
Normal! Normal! Normal!
Katzenjammer, Hooligan, Rah! He! Haw!
Mississippi Normal! Rah! Rah! Rah!

(Cheer quoted in *Normal College News*, 1919).

The 1916 football team included M. M. Roberts (front row, right)

At left, the college orchestra, 1920.

"Blink" Anderson, "Puny" Davis, "Mutt" Campbell, and the Busby boys, "Red" and "Black." M. M. Roberts played on the 1916 squad, while Nollie Felts (1922–24) and D. C. Leech (1923–24) eventually found their way to the University of Southern Mississippi Sports Hall of Fame. Local support was generally dismal, as indicated by the cancellation of the 1923 game with Ole Miss.

Basketball started at MNC on an outdoor court behind Forrest County Hall. In those early days the black and gold played such powers as the D'Lo YMCA, the Richton All-Stars, Chamberlain-Hunt Academy, and the Bogalusa Gaylords. The school did not field a team in 1917 or 1918 because of the World War, and a flu epidemic wiped out the 1920 season. The 1921 squad traveled to the Gulf Coast for a game against the Gulfport Naval Training Center and found themselves playing on a wooden ballroom floor for which they had no suitable footwear. Undaunted, the "teachers" simply smeared their feet with resin and played barefoot, though their heroic perseverance was no match for the "vacuum bottom" sneakers of the sailors who won 53–17. The lack of an indoor playing facility continued to plague the college until the Demonstration School gymnasium opened in 1934. As with football, however, the real problem was lack of

community interest, which led to cancellation of the 1924 season. There was even less interest in other sports, which included volleyball, tennis, track, and women's basketball.

In 1920 Audie F. Fugitt, who then occupied the French horn chair in Miss Lorena Tomson's college orchestra, set out to organize a brass band. Help came from college engineer V. C. Cagle and several other students, including J. W. McCleskey and J. B. George. Using instruments donated by the student body, the all-male group rehearsed in classrooms, basements, the powerhouse, and even the college barn, until a frame band building was constructed in 1924. The band made its first road appearance at the Mississippi Teachers Association convention in Meridian in 1923 and by 1925 was playing for chapel programs, athletic events, rallies, fairs, and other public events. Fugitt, as student and later as faculty member, directed the band for most of its first decade and a half. In 1923 fifteen Mississippi Normal College coeds organized the state's first all-female band, which also began to perform at various functions, including the premiere broadcast of Hattiesburg radio station WCBG. In their ankle-length blue pleated skirts, white coat-sweaters, and black and gold hats, they looked, said President Cook, "real tidy."

The girls' band, 1924.

*A*merica's entry into the Great War in 1917 brought the first major changes to the college. Enrollment dropped sharply as 390 students, along with twelve faculty members, marched away to make the world safe for democracy. Six never returned. On October 12, 1918, the school organized a Student Army Training Corps to train officer candidates. The 102 inductees "certainly looked fine in their new uniforms," the *News* reported, but the war ended just as they "were showing splendid improvement" in their drills. They were mustered out on December 6, after less than two months' service. The influx of 40,000 regular troops at nearby Camp Shelby led to some precautionary modifications in campus discipline. Cook forbade dating between students and soldiers and hired a night watchman and a day guard to keep unauthorized visitors off the grounds. All student courting rites were restricted to the lobbies, even on Sunday afternoon.

The legislature had for years ignored Cook's pleas for funds to build a hospital, so when the world-wide outbreak of influenza hit the campus soon after the war, Cook converted the Industrial Cottage into a hospital. The epidemic, which killed more American soldiers than had German arms

Not So Normal

*T*he postwar frivolity that would characterize America in the 1920s first came to MNC in the form of several unconventional organizations. The Beau Not Club, opposite page, appeared in response to the administrations's wartime restrictions on campus social hours. The club's motto was, "Full many a flower is born to blush unseen and waste its fragrance on the desert air;" its purpose was "consolation and revenge." The Bolshevik Club,

below—only remotely associated with the national "Red Scare" of 1919—aimed "to do as much work as possible to get out of work; to store away knowledge where there is no room; and to furnish information on the values of Campus Course, Volley Ball, Tiddle-de-Wink, and other unnecessary undertakings at the Normal College." The club's color was, of course, red; its song, "Hail! Hail! The Gang's All Here;" its password, "Hunting the Zoo;" and its motto, "Watch Your Step." The Bolsheviks "put on a campaign for 'more beef and less gravy,' [and] voted unanimously that the cooks discontinue washing the mackerel before serving, since water destroys its greatest quality—fragrance." Other exotic organizations included the Jiggs Club, named for a popular comic strip character, and the Bobbed Hair Club.

The "Bolshevik" Club

The campaign to raise funds for a World War Memorial Streetcar Station, below, was headed by A. V. Hays and Kate Brown, insets. The station became home to Rev. and Mrs. W. E. Fail, right, "Ma and Pa" to the students. In addition to caring for the building, Rev. Fail, a Civil War veteran, "guarded the campus at night and chased suspicious automobiles on Sunday."

during the war, claimed no victims at Mississippi Normal College, thanks largely to the heroic efforts of Dr. May F. Jones.

College Secretary A. V. Hays suggested in 1920 that the school erect a campus streetcar station as a memorial to those of the college community who had served during the war. Cook approved and appointed Hays and Kate Brown to direct a campaign to raise funds. Faculty, staff, students, and alumni contributed generously enough to subscribe the necessary $10,000 and lay the cornerstone on July 4, 1921.

Significant changes continued after the war. Enrollment again burgeoned, placing a great strain on facilities. By 1919 there were twenty-three instructors but only thirteen classrooms, forcing manual training classes to meet in the basement of Mississippi Hall. Cook renewed a longstanding request for another academic building, and the legislature finally appropriated the money in 1920. A fully-equipped Science Hall (now Southern Hall), identical to and directly across from College Hall, opened two years later.

Not all the changes were good. In 1922 Cook had to report to the board the first student deaths, one a swimming accident in the Bowie River, the other

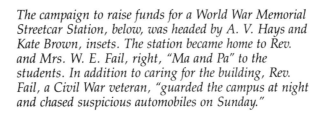

Science Hall (now Southern Hall), as seen from College Hall looking east. The spot across the road (right) from the south entrance to the building is now occupied by Lake Byron.

offered students little more than a review of basic courses in preparation for the state teacher's examination. As the state's education system gradually improved, however, the college was able to stiffen its entrance requirements, accepting only high school graduates after 1917. By 1922 the recitation period was up from 45 minutes to an hour, the certificate requirement from 40 hours to 84, the diploma course from 80 to 150, and the faculty from 18 to 31.

By that time, many normal college graduates found their road to advancement blocked as more and more Mississippi schools required principals to hold degrees. In 1921 the Alumni Association launched an effort to secure legislation allowing the college to offer a baccalaureate program. Representative—and Mississippi Normal College student—M. L. Riley introduced such a bill, which the lawmakers passed in 1922. In May of the same year, Mississippi Normal College took a major step on the long road to academic distinction, awarding its first bachelor of science degree to Kathryn Swetman of Biloxi. As it matured, however, the institution never lost sight of its original vision, to make life richer for the people of Mississippi.

a sudden heart attack. A continuing struggle for adequate funds led to a gradual de-emphasis of agricultural studies. The campus farm was abolished in 1922 and the entire agriculture department in 1930.

There were also several faculty changes. The three-grade practice school went through three different teachers in its first five years. George G. Hurst succeeded Brim, who took a job at Winthrop College in South Carolina in 1915. When Bond became state superintendent of education the following year, Cook appointed H. L. McCleskey to head the history department. Claude S. Hall re-placed Thames, who left in 1916, and O. V. Austin took over science from Slay in 1922. In the 1920s Cook began to encourage faculty members to take leaves of absence to pursue higher degrees, and by 1928 a majority held master's degrees.

Also by the 1920s, the school's success in its original mission was transforming the institution and expanding its academic horizons. From the very beginning Cook had sought to improve the college curriculum enough to justify a formal degree program in education, but the academic background of the early students was simply too poor to allow it. For the first decade, the school in reality

The New Spirit

*I*t is difficult to recapture the mood of passionate optimism that permeated the early years of MNC. Fortunately, Alma Hickman left for posterity a dramatic representation of the institution's early life in the form of a pageant, "Neka Camon," an Indian phrase meaning "new spirit." The three-act production portrayed allegorically "the magical effects," as the campus newspaper described it, "of the Normal College brand of Education," which subdues four grisly figures who appear on stage chanting:

> We are cruel as death and relentless as fate,
> We are Ignorance, Poverty, Disease and Hate;
> With our chains we shall bind your children free
> In the town, on the farm, wherever they be.
> We shall banish the light and bring in the dark,
> All evil spirits we shall enthrone,
> The good cast out, we shall reign, alone.
> We are cruel as death and relentless as fate,
> We are Ignorance, Poverty, Disease, and Hate.

The play included vignettes of Mississippi history beginning with the author herself, in center of photograph, as the Spirit of the Pines rising "gracefully," according to a *Hattiesburg American* reviewer, "above the tall background of green in a magnificent costume, carrying out the symbolism. The stage below teemed with graceful sprites, Pine Needles, opposite page, Red Birds, Blue Birds, and Rabbits . . . cunningly represented by Miss Hooper's Practice School children." The theme of the pageant was the birth of a "New Spirit" to preside over a new temple which the Spirit of Mississippi builds to honor the Spirit of Education. The "New Spirit" is, of course, MNC:

Oh Spirits fair, please tell to me,
What the name of this New Spirit shall be.
(Spirits sing in distance):
  She is Neka Camon, new spirit of knowledge,
  Known to mortals as Normal College.

More than 300 college students participated in the production which was filmed to be shown throughout the state as a promotional feature for the institution. A second live performance in Woodlawn Park on campus drew over 3000 spectators.

Orville Brim, right, was professor of education on the first faculty at MNC. In 1922 Kathryn Swetman, below, of Biloxi received the first degree awarded by MNC.

State Teachers College

1924 - 1940

STATE TEACHERS COLLEGE

Hattiesburg Miss.

Nineteen twenty-four was a pivotal year for Mississippi Normal College. In September the campus newspaper noted that it had been thirteen years since Joe Cook "stepped out on the platform in the auditorium of College Hall, cleared his throat, smiled, and announced the opening of the first session." On Tuesday morning, September 16, the *News* continued, he "stepped out on the same platform and announced the opening of the 14th session of that same institution." Yet it was not precisely the same institution. Still possessing the "same purpose and spirit . . . with which it has been imbued from the very beginning," the school now possessed, thanks to a legislative act of March 7, 1924, a new name, State Teachers College (STC).

The newspaper, which also bore a new name, the *Teachers College News*, reported that the president opened STC "with the same lively step, with the same beam in his eye, and the same smile on his face" as when he opened Mississippi Normal College in 1912. But there was one significant difference, and it was already affecting the school more profoundly than the name change. "President Cook," declared the *News*, "has allowed that 'standardization bug' to get under his shirt."

The comment referred to Cook's determination to conform State Teachers College, as soon as possible, to requirements set by the American Association of Teachers Colleges. Spurred by the difficulty students encountered when seeking to transfer work from the Hattiesburg institution to other colleges, Cook decided that STC must become an accredited teachers college. As a first step toward standardization of the curriculum, the faculty had, in January 1924, recommended a shift to the quarter system.

At the same time, Cook hired Professors Shelton Phelps and Charles A. McMurry of Peabody College in Nashville to conduct an extensive study of the college and recommend whatever changes were necessary to achieve accreditation. Their report, issued in February 1924, focused on three areas: instruction, facilities, and faculty qualifications. A random survey of the records of diploma and degree students revealed several deficiencies. Inadequate classification often placed students with little or no high school training in classes with finishing college students, contributing to a high failure rate among the first group, who were ill prepared for such work, and fruitless repetition of basic college instruction by the second, who should have been doing advanced work. The study

recommended (1) "complete and accurate classification of all students in terms of the accepted methods of evaluating credits . . . recognizing *no exceptions* whatever" and (2) a restructuring of the curriculum, clearly distinguishing high school, junior college, and senior college courses. "For the present," said McMurry, "the main feature in this institution" should be a two-year program to prepare high school graduates to teach in the common schools. The changes, however, would allow for the gradual evolution "into a real not nominal Teachers' College." The report also called for a second vice-president, with a Ph.D. degree from a standard teachers college, to administer instruction according to policies developed by the faculty through appropriate committees. The consultants also endorsed the shift to the quarter system as well as a significant expansion of faculty and courses.

The greatest need, in terms of facilities, said Phelps and McMurry, was for a Training School which should be "a model for consolidated schools," both in structure and in instruction, and should become the focus of the entire process of training teachers. The study also called for additional library equipment, including a minimum of

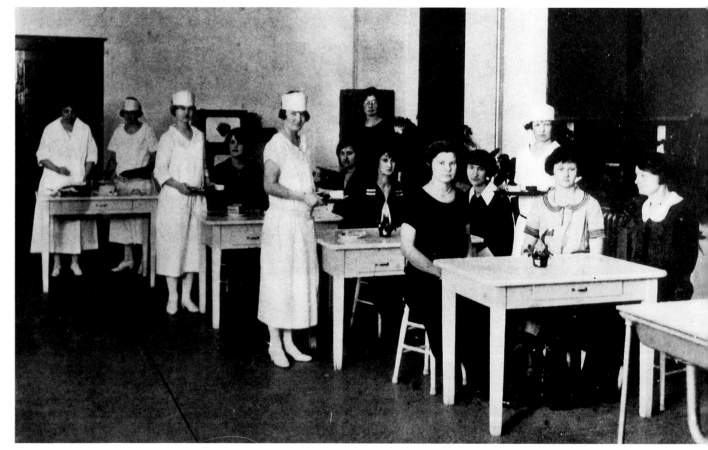

"8000 . . . well distributed, professionally administered volumes," and a fully equipped gymnasium to accommodate "a well organized department of physical education."

Every new faculty member, the consultants suggested, should have at least a master's degree in his field of study as well as a graduate minor in education. The administration should allow existing faculty "every opportunity and encouragement" to attain these standards, including a year's leave of absence at half pay to pursue advanced study. Also, the school should establish a salary schedule based on "training, experience, and teaching efficiency."

In a letter to Cook accompanying the report, Phelps cautioned that standardization was not "an overnight process," but "a matter of evolution" that would take several years. He insisted, however, that many of the suggestions "may be realized at once," allowing State Teachers College to "take its rightful place among all colleges of the state, and among the teachers colleges of the nation. There is no reason," he concluded, "why this cannot be made one of the outstanding teachers colleges of the South." Finally, Phelps offered a tribute to the current faculty, "an earnest determined group,

J. Fred Walker's anatomy class. Professor Walker joined the STC faculty in 1926 and remained for almost half a century.

[whose] spirit . . . causes them to determine upon standardizing everything about the work of the college, even when some do not actually meet the degree requirements of such a college. Sober judgment must give to those who have worked here for the past twelve years the full credit for the splendid progress already made."

Many of the Phelps-McMurry recommendations proved impractical, primarily for financial reasons. There was no money for a vice-president of instruction, and Alma Hickman insisted that she knew of no faculty member who was ever paid a penny during a leave of absence until well into the 1950s. Nonetheless, several of the suggestions were implemented fairly quickly. In the 1924–25 academic year, the school went to a twelve-week quarter system with classes meeting four times each week. Courses of study included a one-year certificate program (48 quarter hours), a two-year certificate program (96 hours), a three-year diploma course (144 hours), and a four-year degree course (192 hours). Renumbered courses reflected clearly defined academic levels: 25–49, freshman; 50–99, sophomore; 100–149, junior; and 150–199, senior. There were 290 courses scattered over 19 departments. The degree requirements included

32 hours of education, 20 of English, and 12 each in foreign language, history, and science. Additional hours for a major, two minors, and electives brought the total to 192. Except for minor modifications, this remained the basic curriculum for more than two decades.

Thanks largely to the efforts of the STC Alumni Association, led by President George McLendon and Secretary J. B. George, a new $125,000 Demonstration School (now the George Hurst Building) opened in September 1927. The first year's appropriation provided for only eight grades, but the addition of four more in 1928 made it a full-grade high school. McLendon became the first principal, and George Hurst, as head of the college's Department of Education, the first director. The recommended gymnasium, which for years would serve the college as well as the Demonstration School, was not completed until 1934.

Convinced by 1927 that the college was ready to pursue accreditation, Cook initiated the process with the proper regional accrediting agency, the Southern Association of Colleges and Secondary Schools. He would not be around to enjoy the outcome. That November Vice-president Scott attended the association's annual meeting in Jack-

sonville, Florida, to file for membership, but regulations required the application to lay over for a year. By the time the group met again, Joe Cook had ended his presidency of State Teachers College as a casualty of Mississippi politics.

The trouble began in 1927 when the state's voters returned former governor Theodore G. Bilbo to the post he had left in 1920. Cook had been an outspoken critic of Bilbo in the past, and by October 1928, the governor had mustered enough support among the board of trustees to remove the president and replace him with Claude Bennett. The firing of Cook foreshadowed a more sweeping Bilbo purge of higher education that would come in 1930, and it marked the end of an era at STC. During its first sixteen years, the institution awarded 2,112 certificates, 752 diplomas, and 248 degrees. Since enrollment had totaled almost 11,000, and many students completed all three programs, some 8,000 students apparently never finished any of the three courses of study. This would seem to substantiate Alma Hickman's assessment that for much of the Cook era, the Normal College gave its students little more than "a review of basic elementary subjects" to prepare them for the state teacher's examinations.

Claude Bennett, below, replaced Joe Cook as president in 1928. The campus in 1927, opposite page, included (from left) College Hall, Forrest County Hall, the old Dining Hall, Mississippi Hall, Hattiesburg Hall, and Science Hall. The pavilion behind Science Hall and an identical one behind College Hall became known as "courting sheds" for obvious reasons.

STUDENT PRINTZ

VOL. II.   Hattiesburg, Miss., October 3, 1928   Number 23

Joe Cook Is Ousted at S. T. C.

Choctaws Down Yellow-jackets, Score 83 to 0

Homelings Outclassed in Opening Game of Season

The Yellowjackets took to the trail last Friday for their first grid tilt of the season, going to Miss. College. Saturday night they came back, a saddened but no less determined team. Although the game Saturday ended disastrously for the Teachers, it should help the players to find themselves, and give Coach Saunders a better insight into the weaknesses as well as the abilities of the individual players. At any rate it is not unsafe to predict that the Yellowjackets will present a changed and vastly stronger line-up when they open hostilities with Perkinston October 5.

The game with Miss. College Saturday was disastrous from the start. Two attempted punts by Bilbo were blocked and converted into touchdowns in the first two minutes of play. This served to demoralize the Teachers and the Choctaws continued to score until they had amassed a total of 83 points. Although the Yellow-jackets were out-classed and out-played in every department of the game, they at times exhibited a bit of real football, occasionally throwing the Choctaw backs for a considerable loss.

Captain Hackney was not in the starting line-up on account of a leg injury received in last week's scrimmaging. He entered later and played a good game. McMahan and Childres also played stellar ball.

We are fortunate in that none of our players received anything more than minor injuries in Saturday's tilt. Especially so since the next game comes on October 5. Much interest is being manifested in the coming game and it is to be hoped that some special arrangement can be made so that those who wish to do so can go with the team to Perkinston. We should at least

Mississippians Enjoy Good Program

Eleven New Members Are Added

Last Friday evening the Mississippians had a very enthusiastic meeting in the lobby of Mississippi Hall with a large number of girls in attendance. The principal feature of the evening's program was an enjoyable talk by Miss Saville, a new member of our faculty. In her talk she told us some very interesting facts about the little town of Fredericksburg, Virginia, which was the home of Mary Washington, mother of the Father of our Country. Miss Saville has had the privilege of working in this historic town and she told us many things about the boyhood home of George Washington and facts concerning his early life there, including some of his love affairs.

At the close of the program the business session was held, the principal item being the installation of officers for this quarter. They are as follows: President, Wilma Smith; vice-president, Eleanor Strange; secretary, Edrie Turner; treasurer, Maymie Fairely; chaplain, Azoline Wells; chorister, Ruth Hargette; reporter, Edna Jones. We were glad to enroll eleven new members at this meeting and offer a cordial invitation to other non-members to come and join us.

SOPHOMORE CONVENTION

Eight o'clock last Tuesday night found the sophomores assembled and ready for action. Not all of the "Wise Fools," were present but there were enough for a real lively meeting. The following officers were elected: Miss Emma Hitt, president; Mr. P. P. Flannigan, vice-president; Mrs. J. C. Everett, secretary; Miss Edna Lee Triplett, treasurer; Mr. O. L. Loper, reporter; Miss Edna Jones, pianist, and Miss Bernice Day, sponsor.

There were many heated debates over the presidential election. The

Simp Jackson Elected Manager

Again students' day in chapel scores success. By an overwhelming majority Simpson Jackson was the choice of S. T. C. students for athletic manager for 1928-29. Mr. Jackson, whose home is in Macon, Miss., and who last year was a star baseball player for S. T. C., but who ruined an ankle in last season's playing, is quite qualified and experienced in athletics. In simpler terms he is the man for the position and with the support of the faculty and student body, athletics in and around S. T. C. are bound to get on the "boom."

There is nothing more stimulating to the college spirit, than good wholesome athletics. They add pep, interest, zeal,, ambition, and friendliness to the constituency of college work. Therefore it is most

(Continued on page 3)

BEST WISHES OF STUDENTS GO WITH MR. JOE COOK

News was received Friday morning that Mr. Cook had been removed from the presidency of the State Teachers College. A committee from the State Teachers College, a committee of students authorized by the student body drew up the following resolutions:

Whereas, Joe Cook has been a friend to education for fifty years.

Whereas, he was instrumental in establishing the State Teachers College.

Whereas, he has served as president of this college for seventeen years.

Whereas, this college has made great progress under his administration, and whereas, through his financial aid and personal interest, he has enabled hundreds of students to secure a college education. Therefore, be it resolved, that the student body of the State Teachers College hereby, expresses its appreciation and gratitude for his unceasing efforts, during his administration.

Be it further resolved, that we

Sherwood Bonners Show Enthusiasm

Sixty Members enrolled.

The Sherwood Bonners "are mild but they satisfy" each other. The society has started off this year with an enrollment of over 60. That is proof that all the freshmen are not so dumb as they are painted, because a good percentage of the members are freshmen. Their elder sisters evidently believe in the old proverb, "Train them up in the way they should go, etc."

Though the Sherwood Bonners feel that they are not being left behind in membership by the other societies, there is a standing invitation to all the co-eds to attend the meetings and join the ranks of the "Literati."

On the evening of Friday, Sept. 21, the society met in the lobby of Hattiesburg Hall, to be entertained by a very enjoyable program. The participants (and their "efforts") were Miss Lessye Karston, a reading, Miss La Velle Morman, a vocal solo, accompanied on the piano by Miss Jonnye Jackson, Miss Eddie Marie Campbell, a violin solo, and Miss Jewel Batte, a reading.

An important business matter was brought up at this meeting. The students will understand just how important when they see all the S. B.'s "strutting" their new pins. The members of their sister society will be easily recognized by

(Continued on page 3)

JUNIORS ELECT OFFICERS

The Junior Class of this institution met Tuesday night of last week for general get-to-gether, and for the purpose of electing officers for this year. The meeting was fairly well attended, and the juniors entered into the business at hand with the pep and enthusiasm that characterized them in the past; as sophomores and even as lowly freshmen. The juniors are expecting a great year's work and among other things expect to make a place for some reasonable privileges for the girls of the class.

Claude Bennett New President Teachers College

Change in Administration Effective October Tenth

The inevitable has come to pass. Pres. Cook has been removed as president of the State Teachers College, a position that he has held for seventeen years. It has been a foregone conclusion that Mr. Cook was to go since R. E. L. Sutherland resigned from the Board of Trustees a few days ago.

Mr. Cook will be succeeded October 10, by Claude Bennett, who is supervisors of rural education in Mississippi.

Mr. Bennett once held position in Hattiesburg High School.

Claude Bennett, president-designate of State Teachers College, has been active in educational work in Mississippi for the past 10 or 12 years. He has been for the past cultural high schools in the State cultural high schools n the State Department of Education, spending part of his time at his home in Clinton and part in Jackson, where his offices are located.

Mr. Bennett was born in Copiah county, and after attending the grammar schools there, he went to Mississippi College at Clinton. He did not finish, but obtained his B. A. degree at Trinity College, now known as Duke University, at Durham, N. C.

Shortly after his graduation he became county superintendent of schools in Lincoln county. After teaching school in a number of places he then came to Hattiesburg where he was principal of the high school for two years. Later he became vice-president of the Mississippi Womans' College, then spent two years as principal at Perkinston Junior College. From there he went to Biloxi as city superintendent of schools. He then became superintendent of high schools in the state department of education.

A few years ago he went to Pea-

Nonetheless, Hickman concluded, "Joe Cook could leave the president's office . . . with his head held high," confident, as he stated in his final report to the board, that "this institution from the beginning . . . has been, and is, fulfilling its mission." A few months before Cook's ouster, STC alumnus Martin L. Riley completed at Peabody College a master's thesis examining the career patterns of State Teachers College graduates. "It is obvious," he concluded, "that a very large majority of graduates go into the teaching service"—most of them in rural schools—"and continue in the profession over a period of time. It is evident that the MSTC is carrying out the purpose for which it was established—namely, to train teachers for the public schools of the state, especially for the rural public schools." Cook "never gave a written contract," said Hickman, "but for sixteen years he gave the faculty an almost perfect security. . . . He was honest, fair-dealing, fearless, and a treasured friend to all who worked with him."

While no one could dispute the enormity of Cook's contribution, the acclaim for the first president was not quite so universal as Alma Hickman suggests. During the legislative debate over changing the school's name in 1924, Representative J. V. Gibson of Lauderdale County read on the floor of the house, a letter, allegedly from a member of the student body, suggesting that Cook was "getting old and . . . losing the respect and confidence of many of the most influential students." Though the student body and faculty voted officially to repudiate the letter's accusations, there is little doubt that many students, and some faculty, chafed under the rigor of Cook's discipline.

Sometime in 1926 there appeared on campus a clandestine force of student resistance and psychological terror that scandalized the institution for months. The movement almost certainly included several students, but the conspirators always left a singular and ominous mark of identity: "The Blackbird." Sidewalks, walls, and especially the water tower offered convenient blank space for the paint brush of protest and defiant sloganeering. The age and marital status of several faculty members became favorite topics of comment. Anna Roberts recalled the shock of exiting the dining hall after breakfast one morning to find "The March of the Dead" scrawled across the sidewalk, and under-

neath, the names of three prominent elderly professors. More startling was the reference to a not-so-young female instructor as the "Last Rose of Summer" splashed in mercilessly bright, painted letters across the front of College Hall. Most shocking of all was the cry of "Down With Pimps" emblazoned upon the water tower and visible from virtually any spot on campus. For Librarian Roberts, who considered herself "more or less a classicist," the implication of the word pimp was only too clear, and she sternly upbraided one of the boys whom she suspected for insinuating such things in public. Her rebuke seemed lost on the young rebel, who artlessly insisted, "The campus is full of them." Her rage then transcended all bounds until the young man finally explained that a pimp was simply an informer, a squealer, a collaborator with the administration. At times the rebellion manifested some unsettling overtones. "You would be walking along the campus, said Roberts, "and all of a sudden . . . put your hand in the pocket of your sweater and . . . find a note signed, 'The Blackbird.'" Another faculty member, noting the proximity of the protest campaign to Cook's departure, guessed that "the Blackbird did have quite a bit to do with it. At least [he] put on a lot of public

pressures."

More likely it was the infamous "Dread Scott" decision of November 1926 that really brought the public's attention to student discontent. The Honor Council of the Student Self-government Association convicted several boys, including one of the vice-president's sons, of drinking on campus and recommended their suspension. When Cook rejected the recommendation and exonerated young Edd Scott, the entire Council resigned in protest. Thereafter, all discipline cases were handled exclusively by the administration, ending fourteen years of student self-government, though the student body continued to elect honorary officers. The controversy found its way into the local newspapers and heightened public awareness of growing student discontent with the administration.

Thus, not all among the campus community were sorry to see President Cook go. One professor saw a certain symbolism in Bennett's early removal of the fence that had surrounded the campus for a decade and a half, declaring, "He really unlocked the prison gates" and ushered in "a new day" for the college. "It was like coming out of the middle ages." Still, Cook remained very popular

From the 1926 yearbook.

The dome of the Administration Building housed a large flood lamp and forty smaller lights reflecting through colored glass windows to cast a soft glow that could be seen for miles.

with most people, and Bennett wore the albatross of Bilbonic politics throughout his tenure. The association with the new governor did, however, carry with it certain advantages, not the least of which was an outpouring of long-needed appropriations that funded a massive construction program. In addition to the Demonstration School, the college added an auditorium (later named for Bennett), the Administration Building, a dining hall (now the Hub), and a home science nursery school (later named for Bertha Fritzsche), all designed by State Architect Vinson Smith, Jr., of Gulfport, who also designed Bilbo's "Dream House" in Pearl River County. Smith's buildings, according to Ed Polk Douglas, comport quite well with Hunt's original design, though on a compressed scale, and "are possibly the handsomest on campus."

The gravel driveways around the campus loop were paved in 1929, and the following year Bennett hired a horticulturist, Albert Leggett, to improve the campus landscape. Soon azaleas began to blossom where pea patches had reigned before, and other flowers and shrubs appeared around the campus. About the same time, the history department designed an elaborate landscape map of Mississippi, 186 feet wide and 330 feet long, with a three-inch-wide concrete boundary and scale model replicas of historic buildings. Covering one-eighth of an acre in front of College Hall, it was to have a flowing stream on the west side to represent the Mississippi River and white sand for the Gulf on the south. Paved walkways lined with shrubbery were to represent the Spanish Trail, Three-Chopped Way, and Natchez Trace. Considerably less sophisticated than originally intended, the project was still quite impressive and took almost three years to complete.

The classes of 1929, 1930, and 1932 jointly sponsored construction of a formal, decorative sunken garden. Dedicated on Class Day in the spring of 1932, it occupied the spot where McLemore Hall now stands. Also that year, the college finally built its own athletic facility, thanks largely to Hattiesburg's Central Committee on Unemployment Relief under Chairman L. E. Faulkner. Week by week, more than 300 casualties of the Depression, unemployed workers of all kinds—college graduates, mechanics, railroad men, plumbers, preachers, and multitudes of day laborers—swapped their labor for a modest allotment of groceries. On October 29, at Homecoming, Mississippi's First Lady, and STC alumna, Mrs. Alma Graham Conner, dedicated the new stadium, named Faulkner

The new Dining Hall (now the Hub) was completed in 1931.

Several of the construction projects of the 1930s, including the Sunken Garden, below, and Lake Byron, opposite page, employed relief labor financed by various New Deal agencies.

Field in honor of the relief committee chairman. Relief labor also contributed to the construction of another campus landmark, Lake Byron, named for Byron Green, President of the Forrest County Board of Supervisors, who helped secure enough federal relief funds to finance the work. The small picturesque pond with an island in the center was a project of the class of 1934. With materials donated by Newman Lumber Company and Hattiesburg Creosote Company, Professor C. E. Thomas's advanced industrial arts class added a scenic arching bridge connecting the island with the mainland.

Bennett, despite the unsavory circumstances of his selection, eventually won acceptance and respect from most students and faculty. He was, after all, well qualified for the post, holding a bachelor's degree from Mississippi College and a master's from Peabody. He had served as vice-president of Mississippi Woman's College, superintendent of the Biloxi school system, and state supervisor of rural schools. Bennett was kind and humane, almost to a fault. His administration encompassed the worst years of the Depression, and his compassionate indulgence of poor students, buffeted by hard times and unable to pay their fees, contrib-

*The Sunken Garden occupied the spot between Science
Hall and President's Home, below, on which McLemore
Hall was later constructed.*

uted, along with general economic conditions, to significant budget problems for the school.

Through most of the lean years, the college was able to pay salaries on schedule, thanks largely to the resourcefulness of Business Manager Clarence Woods. In 1932, however, the state hit bottom. As historian John Ray Skates described it, "mortgages were foreclosed on one of every ten farms in Mississippi. On a single day in April 1932, one-fourth of the land area of Mississippi" passed under the auctioneer's gavel for unpaid taxes. Bilbo left office that year in the same personal financial status in which he had entered it—broke. He was always, in his own words, "poor as Job's turkey." Unfortunately he left the state treasury in the same condition. His successor, Mike Conner, inherited a mere $1326.47 of unencumbered funds. Banks refused credit to state institutions, and for six months state employees, including STC faculty, received no paychecks. The people of Hattiesburg came to the rescue. Banks eased loan policies, and stores extended generous credit. "Old clothes," said Alma Hickman, "were passed around and even became fashionable. Despite the difficulties, we all lived through the winter of our discontent. Spring came, and though our checks did not, there

was talk in the air of passing a sales tax . . . hope was in the air." Conner did steer through the reluctant legislature a sales tax that by the end of the year restored the state's fiscal integrity.

All the problems were not financial. Bennett and Scott renewed the school's application to the Southern Association, which finally admitted State Teachers College to full membership in 1929. The very next year, however, Bilbo gained control of the board that governed the University of Mississippi, Mississippi A&M, and MSCW and extended his purge to those institutions. The association promptly revoked the membership of those three schools, along with that of STC. One victim of Bilbo's renewed vigor was Scott, whose post the board abolished in 1930.

Despite the turmoil, Bennett was able to achieve a measure of academic progress. Beginning in 1928–29, the degree curriculum distinguished separate courses of study for lower elementary, upper elementary, and high school teacher training. In 1929 the diploma program was abolished and a new Department of Correspondence and Extension created, offering classes in twenty-five Mississippi counties. The same year, W. H. Weathersby took over the education department

J. B. George became the school's third president in 1933.

and demonstration school following the sudden death of George Hurst, and STC opened the state's first college-operated nursery school. Also in 1929 Bennett established the office of dean of instruction, which the board ratified the following year. Dr. J. Lawrence Eason was the first to occupy the new post, but when he left after a very brief tenure, Bennett appointed Colley F. Sparkman. In 1930 the board approved the new president's recommendation to place all teachers on nine-month salaries, with every third summer off for advanced study, and authorized the college to grant degrees in music. To head the music department, Bennett hired Frank E. Marsh, Jr., a graduate of the New England Conservatory of Music, who came to STC in 1930 with a master's degree from Syracuse University. He would remain until 1961. By the end of Bennett's presidency in 1933, the institution had awarded 2146 certificates, 768 diplomas, and 905 degrees. Total enrollment for the first twenty years was 27,982, with 14,318 different students attending the college.

In 1932 the legislature placed all of the state's colleges under a single new Board of Trustees of Institutions of Higher Learning. Governor Conner served as ex-officio chairman and appointed all

nine of the other members to staggered terms. The new board immediately reestablished the office of vice-president at STC and filled it with alumnus J. B. George, who had recently earned a Ph.D. degree from Peabody. The board also made overtures to the Southern Association regarding readmission of the Mississippi schools, and by the end of 1933 the association had restored State Teachers College to full accreditation. The new board was designed to eliminate politics from higher education in Mississippi. But before the trustees launched themselves on the road to academic integrity, they disposed of one unfinished bit of blatant political business: they sacked Claude Bennett.

On July 1, 1933, Jennings Burton George became State Teachers College's third chief executive, the first to hold a terminal degree. He had served as both principal and superintendent in Mississippi schools and taught math at State Teachers College and education at Blue Mountain College. Since returning to Hattiesburg in 1932, he had been registrar as well as vice-president. When he moved up, Mary Pulley took over the registrar's

post—which she would retain until her retirement in 1952—and the vice-president's office again disappeared.

The Depression immediately confronted George with a host of pressing problems, but he "proved to be," in Alma Hickman's words, "a frugal businessman and wise administrator." Some of those affected by his austere, but necessary, policies might have described him differently. Among his first economy measures were reductions in employee salaries and increases in student fees. By 1935 a year at STC cost $246, not including books. The annual budget for the library, which had grown to occupy the entire first floor of Science Hall, stagnated at $1800 for a dozen years, prompting Anna Roberts to pronounce George "very economically minded" but not very "library minded."

Frank E. Marsh, Jr., headed the school's music department from 1930 to 1961.

The rise in student expenses and the rapid growth of the state's junior colleges, three of which were within fifty miles of Hattiesburg, forced the college to continue its academic development in order to compete for students. The bulk of that task fell to R. G. Lowrey, who replaced Sparkman as dean in 1934. He immediately organized the various departments into seven divisions: health, language and literature, music, natural sciences and mathematics, practical and fine arts, professional arts, and social studies. The catalog listed 337 courses taught by a faculty of fifty. With faculty approval, Lowrey also instituted a quality point system for grading: three points for an A, two for B, and one for C. He also established a system of academic honors and an elaborate guidance program that included a freshman orientation course, student testing, and frequent faculty-student conferences.

Outside the academic sphere, George's major accomplishment, according to Hickman, was "his fight for morality and honesty. He worked harder on these problems than all others." Some thought he worked too hard. In this he resembled Joe Cook, whose devoted disciple he was. George's inaugural address began with a tribute to his mentor. "The first seventeen years of this institution," he said, "were presided over by a great and good man." There followed a very Cook-like statement on institutional discipline. "I do not believe," the new president declared,

> that any school has a right to exist that does not have a high standard of morality and honesty among its faculty, officers, and students. No faculty member, officer, or student will be permitted to remain at State Teachers College, so long as I am president, who does not have this high standard of morality and honesty. Academic training is good, but academic training without manhood or womanhood is worthless. It shall be our policy to do our best to instill into the young lives of the boys and girls who attend our college that there is something greater in life than academic training.

George's "approach to education developed into many idiosyncrasies which alienated many peo-

ple," said Alma Hickman. Another faculty member put it more bluntly: "George was a puritanical Baptist." A month into his first session as president, George announced to the student body at chapel that there would be "no more leisurely strolling about on remote sections of campus after dark." All "promenading" was thereafter restricted to the area between the main buildings which was "sufficiently illuminated for propriety" and could be easily patrolled by campus police. Students chafed under George's regimen as they had under Cook's. Several nights after the chapel announcement, according the campus newspaper, someone painted on the stadium, "in concise slang," a stern criticism of the new administration. Student body leaders called a special meeting to discuss the issue. Acknowledging that most students had wanted Bennett to remain, student president Reed Green urged the students, nonetheless, to support the new man, which they did with a censure of the prank and a resounding vote of confidence in George.

Campus life was not, in fact, altogether barren, despite the reinvigorated social code. In the fall of 1933, the old laundry building was converted into a student social center, with a college store and

lounge on the top floor and a barbershop in the basement. The store, operated by student workers, sold all school supplies except books, with the profits going to the athletic program. The black and gold decorated lounge contained tables and chairs, free telephones and newspapers, a radio, games, electric fans, and gas heaters. The student body sponsored a contest to name the facility. After a faculty committee pared the ninety-five nominations down to five, the students chose "Yellow Jackets' Nest"—Yellowjackets had become the athletic teams' nickname sometime in the mid-twenties—in a special chapel referendum. Sara Weathersby and Kathryn Simmons, who had submitted the winning name, split the grand prize of $2.50 worth of store goods. The center was open until ten o'clock every night except Sunday.

In front of the building sat the old band hall, which had also housed the old barbershop. The college Golf Association now acquired this wooden frame structure for a clubhouse and moved it to the recently opened nine-hole course just west of the campus. The band shifted its activities elsewhere.

Religion remained a central aspect of student life. In 1930 President Bennett established a department of christian education, under campus YMCA secretary Henry T. Ware, to supervise all religious and social functions of the student body. Two years later Ware invited to campus the noted black chemist and fellow of the Royal Academy of Sciences, George Washington Carver. "We feel very fortunate indeed," said Ware, "to be able to present him to our students." Other prominent speakers and performers brought to campus by various organizations included Nelson Eddy, the Vienna Boys Choir, and University of North Carolina sociologist Howard Odum.

In 1934 the campus Christian organizations sponsored Religious Emphasis Week, a program of spiritual activities highlighted by morning and evening sermons Sunday through Friday. This modernized version of an interdenominational campus revival became an annual tradition that continued into the 1960s. Also in 1934 the YMCA, with financial help from campus nurse Beedie Smith, built Pinehaven Lodge (now part of the married student housing complex) as a meeting facility for campus religious and social groups.

Under President George, a Student Christian Federation replaced the Y associations and in the fall of 1937 took over operation of the campus

The old Laundry, above, (later part of the Industrial Arts and ROTC Building) was converted into a student center in 1934. A sandwich shop, top photo, named Wimpy's after the Popeye cartoon character, was added in 1937.

By the late twenties, life at STC included most aspects of the traditional college experience, including freshman hazing.

store. The new proprietors added a pool table, a nickelodeon, and a sandwich shop named Wimpy's after the hamburger-eating Popeye cartoon character. When a new library opened in January 1940, the entire religious-social center moved into the first floor of Science Hall, and the music department occupied the old laundry building.

As the school grew, student life began to take on the trappings of a typical four-year college, including the hazing of freshmen. By the early thirties, all first-year males faced the annual head-shaving ritual as well as the dreaded dispensation of campus equity by the infamous "Court of Permanent Inter-class Justice." This kangaroo court summoned its accused in a fashion fitting the vermin whose title each freshman bore. "Like the piper of old," said the campus newspaper, "the Judge raps and rats come tumbling, some grumbling, but the worst is yet to come." The highlight of one "rather full docket" was the case of Rats Calender and Therman, who were accused of intelligence, "a serious charge for a rat." The tribunal, after very brief deliberation, declared the defendants patently innocent and sentenced them to debate the proposition, "A nut is not what it is cracked up to be." Their performance, of course, proved a thor-

ough vindication of the court, leaving "no doubt . . . as to the correctness of the verdict." Their punishment appears rather mild in light of the correspondent's none-too-subtle report that before adjournment, "the upper classmen reduced the seating capacity of some ten freshmen. At the next session, Judge Tumlin promises much weeping and wailing and fanning of seats."

The newspaper, which was now entirely a student enterprise, changed its name in 1927 to the *Student Printz.* The change, according to former editor O. B. Brewer, grew out of a meeting that he and other students interested in improving the publication held in T. P. Scott's classroom in College Hall. After the group had rejected several possibilities, Brewer glanced at the label on his pipe, Student Prince, and suggested that it might make a good title. Alma Hickman, who was also present, liked the sound of the phrase and pointed out that it was also the title of a popular contemporary musical. The group decided to present the idea to the student body, and in a campus referendum the new name won approval, though not without serious opposition. The campus newspaper has been the *Student Printz* ever since. The yearbook, called *Neka Camon* after 1920, did not

fare so well. It suspended publication after 1931, a victim of Depression era finances, and did not appear again until 1938.

Other activities and organizations, however, flourished throughout most of the STC years. In 1926 the twenty-four piece college band traveled with the Know Mississippi Better train on an extensive tour of the eastern United States and Canada that included a parade down Manhattan's Fifth Avenue and a performance at the Palace Theater. For four years Audie Fugitt's group was the official band for this annual traveling exhibition of Mississippi boosterism, which took them eventually into almost every state in the union as well as to Canada and Mexico. To raise money for these trips,

the young musicians played such events as the Picayune Peach Carnival, the Hattiesburg Water Carnival, and Trades Day fairs in Sumrall, Richton, Wiggins, and New Augusta.

Audie Fugitt's departure in 1929, along with a Depression budget—the administration even sold its musical instruments to raise money—left the school without a band for a year. In the fall of 1930, however, the college hired a new director, Dewey W. Camp, who reorganized the band in time to perform under the direction of seventy-six year old John Philip Sousa, whose sixty-piece band appeared on campus on October 23. During the thirties the band, under Camp, Fugitt (who returned 1933–36), and William Morgan Keller (1936–43), appeared at Mardi Gras in New Orleans, United Confederate Veterans conventions in Montgomery and Richmond, the Chicago World's Fair, and the inauguration of President Franklin D. Roosevelt in Washington, in addition, of course, to STC football games and other local events.

Other musical programs flourished, as Frank Marsh began to develop music into one of the college's stronger departments. In 1930 he organized the A Capella Choir, which became the Vesper Choir a year later. Soon afterward Marsh initiated

The STC Band traveled throughout the United States, Canada, and Mexico with the "Know Mississippi Better" Train in the late 1920s.

"Picture taken at Washington Monument. D.C. "Know Mississippi Better" Train enroute through Eastern States and Canada August 12 - 31, 1926. Lieut. Gov. Dennis Murphree, Gen. Chairman A.F. Fugitt, Band Director.

1. A.F. Fugitt
2. P.L. Thomas
3. Gabrielle Anderson
4. D.S. Hall
5. L.T. Hinton
6. J.E. Hulett, Jr.
7. Beula Stockton
8. H.H. Mellard
9. C.F. Dodson
10. D.W. Camp
11. H.L. Gillespie
12. E.E. Cook
13. S.J. Ingram
14. Mildred East
15. J.P. Moseley
16. Gladys Turrittin
17. J.W. McCleskey
18. C.E. Craft
19. Lula Mae Moore
20. Bessie Rivers
21. A.H. Blackwell
22. I.A. Saucier
23. H. Lynn McCleskey

Frank Marsh conducts the traditional Christmas presentation of Handel's Messiah.

an annual tour that took the young singers into schools and churches throughout the state, generating good will for the college and exhibiting the quality of its musical program. In 1932 the choir joined with the Hattiesburg Choral Union to present what would become another annual college tradition, the December performance of Handel's *Messiah.*

Sometime in 1934 another basic element of college life came to the school when seven male students organized the XXX Club to "bring about closer fellowship among the fellowmen of State Teachers College." In February of the following year, the club became Kappa Alpha Tau, the college's first social fraternity. Next came Kappa Phi Sigma, which changed to Delta Sigma in 1941 to become the first affiliate of a national fraternity on campus. By that time the college had five sororities, two of them with national affiliation. Sigma Theta Kappa was the first local group, organized in early 1936, followed by Mu Omega a year later. The third local group, Gamma Delta Tau, petitioned to join Sigma Sigma Sigma, and in May 1937, became STC's first national sorority. Alpha Sigma Alpha followed shortly thereafter, accepting

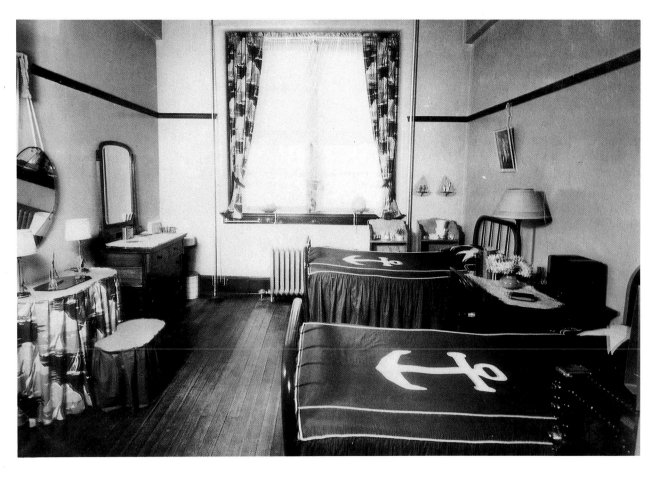

The home science nursery, above, (now part of the Bertha Fritzsche Home Economics Building) was completed in 1930. At left, a women's dormitory room in the 1930s.

Legalized dancing, opposite page, finally came to STC in 1940. At left, M-Club initiation, 1938.

another local sorority, Beta Sigma, into its national organization. The fifth women's group was a local sorority, Delta Sigma, founded in 1938.

The advent of a campus Greek community intensified the already mounting pressure on the administration to relax its restriction against dancing. In January 1940 President George finally yielded to the relentless forces of modernity, but it was largely a tactical retreat. "All dances," said the new regulations, "shall be given for the social welfare of students, faculty, and officers of State Teachers College." Groups could sponsor dances only on Friday nights and had to provide two faculty or staff chaperones. Women students could not leave the premises without permission, and non-students could not attend.

Having sanctioned formal dances for fraternities and sororities, the administration could hardly withhold the privilege from others. There was, therefore, a separate code for "informal dancing," which was permitted during designated hours on Monday, Tuesday, Thursday, and Friday afternoons and evenings. Participants again had to provide chaperones, who were to insure that all dancing was "in accord with grace and rhythm and in every respect in good taste."

In a stroke of peculiar irony, the new regulations went into effect barely a month before the death of Joe Cook. It is doubtful that the first president would ever have countenanced any kind of dancing, tasteful or otherwise. But when dancing did come to State Teachers College, Cook's ghost was there to regulate it. Rule number nine stated: "Each young man attending a dance shall conduct himself as a gentleman, and each young woman . . . shall conduct herself as a lady."

During the STC years, the institution began to emerge as a serious competitor in college football, though not before suffering several more embarrassments, including a 38–6 thrashing at the hands of the Ole Miss freshmen in the midst of an 0–6 campaign in 1925. Herschel Bobo coached the Yellowjackets from 1924 to 1927, compiling a 9–17–4 record. W. B. Saunders (1928–29) and John Lumpkin (1930–31) followed. The first real success came with former Alabama all-American Pooley Hubert (1932–36), who led the team to a 24–19–5 record during his five seasons. The five victories in 1932, the most in any season in the school's history to that point, were highlighted by a crucial Thanksgiving Day game against Union University of Jackson, Tennessee. A young back from Greene

County known as the "Leakesville Express" provided the turning point in that final game of that pivotal season. To the delight of 2000 fans in the newly dedicated Faulkner Field, Reed Green raced eighty-one yards for a fourth-quarter touchdown to seal a 6–0 STC victory. It was a portent of success. Over the next forty years, Reed Green, as player, coach, and athletic director, would lead the school's athletic program to national distinction. After graduating in 1934, Green became an assistant coach and eventually replaced Hubert, who in 1937 accepted a position at Virginia Military Institute. Green hired as his assistant a young Meridian high school coach and former Ole Miss team captain named Thad Vann. These two, Reed Green and "Pie" Vann, would soon construct a football power in Hattiesburg.

The college took a major step toward solving its perennial scheduling problem by joining the Southern Intercollegiate Athletic Association in December 1930. Thereafter, only four-year colleges appeared on the schedule. The construction of Faulkner Field in 1932 was another major step, enhanced by the addition of lights two years later and a public address system in 1937. In 1938 construction began on a stadium dormitory. Financed

Coach Pooley Hubert

Yellowjacket Football

Above left, USM Sports Hall of Fame member "Coon" Leach; left, East Stadium; above, Coach Reed Green (left) and assistant Pie Vann.

by federal public works funds and college revenue bonds, East Stadium opened in time for the football season of 1939.

Despite the increasing respectability of its football program, the college continued to struggle for support. In 1926 the Alumni Association recommended abolishing football. By the 1930s, however, both the alumni and the people of Hattiesburg were beginning to recognize that a successful athletic program could be an asset to the college and to the community. The Alumni Association established an athletic advisory council in 1929, and in 1937 several Hattiesburg civic leaders organized the "500" Club to promote STC athletics. These efforts helped the football program to thrive, but other sports continued to lag far behind.

College Hall, below, as seen from Science Hall, 1939. The space between Science Hall and Hattiesburg Hall, left, just in front of the campus hospital (later the Honor House) would soon be occupied by the new Joe Cook Memorial Library.

By the end of the 1930s, it was obvious that the college was becoming more than a teacher training institute. In an ironically prescient comment, President George reminded a state legislator in early 1940 that State Teachers College was the only public "senior college in the southern two-thirds of the state. This being true, we have a great part of the state to serve." Surely George could not have known just how true that statement was about to become. The cataclysm that had erupted only a few months before, halfway around the world in Poland, would soon work a profound transformation over the entire face of the globe. The tremors would shake even Mississippi, where they produced changes that, though quite modest when compared to dislocations elsewhere, were significant enough, both for the state and for its expanding teachers college. The southward drift of Mississippi's population had begun well before 1940, but World War II helped turn it into a flood. Workers poured into South Mississippi for jobs created by large military installations at Camp Shelby and Keesler Field in Biloxi and the huge shipbuilding complex at Pascagoula. Money poured in, too, shifting the state's economic center of gravity southward as well. After the war thousands of veterans returned, many of them eager to begin or resume college educations delayed by military service.

By 1940 the demographic changes were already affecting State Teachers College. For South Mississippi's growing population, it was becoming the logical place to pursue higher education. While "many boys and girls," as one supporter of the college observed, "avoid going to the school because they don't plan to teach," enough STC students were preparing for non-teaching careers that by 1938 the curriculum included pre-professional training in dentistry, medicine, pharmacy, law, and engineering. The following year the board of trustees voted to allow the school to offer a bachelor of arts degree.

Not everyone, however, appreciated the value of the college. Thirty-six representatives co-sponsored in the 1934 legislature a bill to abolish State Teachers College. Two years later, a senate bill proposed to make the Hattiesburg school a southern branch of the University of Mississippi. Both bills died in committee, but they underscored the precarious nature of STC's existence and convinced the administration and its friends that another name change was essential, both to protect the institution and to reflect its expanding mission. "You know and I know," George wrote to a state senator from Forrest County, "that we are training many people who never expect to teach. . . . If we are to render the service that is demanded of us, we must have the name changed."

Again, however, progress did not come at the expense of the institution's original vision. Bell Wiley perhaps best expressed the spirit of that vision as it endured through the STC era. Wiley first taught at the college in the summers of 1930 and 1931. Three years later he returned, with a fresh Ph.D. degree from Yale University, to head the history department. In 1938 he left again and went on to establish a remarkably distinguished career that included professorships at the University of Mississippi, Louisiana State University, and Emory University, as well as visiting professorships at the University of Southern California and Tulane University. In 1965–66, Wiley was Harmsworth Professor of History at Oxford University. But his years at State Teachers remained special. "As I look back on it," he later said,

> I think maybe that I got more real satisfaction out of teaching during my four years and two summers there than I did at any other place or time

At left, librarian Anna Roberts and history professor Bell Wiley. In 1940 the library moved from Science Hall, opposite page, to a new facility, below, named for former president Joe Cook.

in my teaching career. . . . The satisfaction derived mainly from the fact that you could see, in a rather startling way, the results of your teaching. You could see these young men and young women come to you unscrubbed from the sandy hills of south Mississippi and take on culture, and you could realize that you were having a part in that. . . . My main concern in history has been the lowly people, the country people, partly because I grew up among them. They are unassuming; they are modest; they are open to suggestion. . . . Many of [these young people] were eager. They wanted to improve themselves. It was fun to be with them.

Perhaps it was the closeness, spatially and otherwise, between faculty and students that nurtured this spirit. Anna Roberts, like Bell Wiley, lived in a dormitory with students during those years. On first coming to campus, she later recalled, "I . . . took up my residence on the third floor of Hattiesburg Hall, something for which I always—and I stress always—have been very thankful. It was . . . that way that I learned to know so well and appre-

ciate so much the many faculty members and students. . . . I lived there in that dormitory for thirteen years and had the time of my life."

Librarian Roberts had another vivid memory from the 1930s, near the very end of the State Teachers College era. During the Christmas holidays of 1939, the 22,250 volumes under her care "were transferred through snow and sleet" to a brand new Library. Built with New Deal Public Works Administration funds, it was a "two story brick building with four identical reading rooms, a large rotunda with eight massive columns supporting a lighted dome, a stack area, and several offices." The new building represented, the *Student Printz* declared, "more than a quarter of a century's efforts and work in one of the most important departments of the College." It was a concrete expression of the quest for academic distinction and bore the name of the school's first president. As the Joseph Anderson Cook Library, it stood as a fitting symbol of the institution's continuing union of heritage and progress.

Silver Jubilee

State Teachers College marked its twenty-fifth anniversary in May 1937, with a three-day celebration that included speeches, receptions, garden parties, an alumni reunion, and a huge parade through downtown Hattiesburg. Helen Wright of Raymond was elected Jubilee Queen, and Ole Miss Chancellor A. B. Butts delivered the commencement address. "The purpose of these Jubilee programs," said President George, "is to rally all the citizens of Mississippi in honor of the anniversary of an outstanding event in the history of public education in Mississippi. . . .

Those who have directed this institution from the day it was founded have held to the conviction that the only hope of salvation in our democracy is in the high quality of our citizenship, that the most vital and constructive force in citizenship is the public school, and that, in turn, the most vital element in the public school is the well-prepared teacher."

Silver Jubilee Edition
Student Printz

Student Publication Of Mississippi State Teachers College

VOLUME X   HATTIESBURG, MISS., WEDNESDAY, MAY 19, 1937   Number 30

Jubilee Jubilee Jubilee

S. T. C. Celebrates Full Quarter Century of Worthy Educational Service to State

Past Presidents State Teachers

W. H. SMITH

W. H. Smith enjoys the distinction of being the first nominal head of State Teachers College, although he never saw any service in actual administration. He was head of the educational set-up when Mississippi Normal College was created by the State Legislature in 1912. For many years he served as executive secretary of the Board of Trustees of Higher Learning. At present Mr. Smith is president and treasurer of the National Hospital Insurance Corporation, Jackson, Mississippi.

JOE COOK

Joe Cook was the first active president of State Teachers College. This position as executive head of S. T. C. climaxed years of educational service in the schools of the state. He graduated from Vanderbilt University, was head of the schools at Artesia, Mississippi, was ten years superintendent of the city schools of Columbus, and served as president of State Teachers Association in 1907. His term as president of State Teachers College lasted from 1912, when the college, as such, opened its doors for the first time, until 1928. Under his administration the college knew progress and growth. Today Joe

DR. J. B. GEORGE

The present executive responsibility of State Teachers College rests with Dr. J. B. George. Dr. George has been president of the institution since 1933. He is a true son of S. T. C. having received his B. S. degree from here in 1923. His higher training represents work at George Peabody College and the University of Chicago. The recognition the College has received and the phenomenal progress it has made under his leadership are living testimonials of the quiet, direct efficiency of his

Lokey Awarded Scholarship

E. B. Lokey, Jr., who was graduated from S. T. C. in 1936, was one of the four Mississippians to receive a four-year medical scholarship through the commonwealth fund, a philanthropic foundation in New York, to the Tulane University School of Medicine.

There are four of these scholarships awarded annually to deserving medical students from Mississippi as an aid to better rural health service.

The Mississippi State Board of Health and the School of Medicine at Tulane together decide upon the recipients of the awards.

DR. A. B. BUTTS

Dr. A. B. Butts, Chancellor of the University of Mississippi, will deliver the principal address at the annual Commencement Exercises, Tuesday evening, May twenty-fifth, at eight o'clock, college auditorium.

Students, Faculty, Alumni and Citizens of State Join in Colorful Jubilee Events

Helen Wright Elected Queen

Miss Helen Wright, senior, of Raymond, was elected queen of the Silver Jubilee Celebration by the faculty and student body in chapel Monday, May 17. Miss Wright has twice been elected "Miss S. T. C." and received this year a unanimous nomination among the classes for "most beautiful girl."

The four maids to serve with Miss Wright in the Jubilee Court are: Miss Chlyce Page, Monticello; Miss Katie Ruth Field, Magee; Miss Beulah Kent, Klinkchari; and Miss Katherine Saunders, Meridian.

These young ladies will be honored in the festival parade and at the buffet supper Tuesday, May 25.

FOREWORD

The purpose of these Jubilee programs is to rally all the citizens of Mississippi in honor of the anniversary of an outstanding event in the history of public education in Mississippi. In this, our Silver Jubilee year at State Teachers College, through appropriate ceremonies, we pay tribute to the founders and builders of this, the first state-owned teacher-training institution in Mis-

Twenty-five years of educational service to Mississippi is the occasion for State Teachers College's gala celebration. The progress and growth of the institution from the opening of its doors in 1912 to the magnitude of the college as it stands today will be depicted through speeches, receptions, parades, and alumni visits beginning Sunday, May 23rd, and climaxing with Silver Jubilee Commencement Exercises, May 25th.

The program for the anniversary activities is as follows:

Sunday, May 23rd
11:00 a. m.—Baccalaureate Sermon Reverend John Lloyd Decell, D. D. Pastor, Galloway Memorial M. E. Church, South, Jackson Miss. College Auditorium
6:30 p. m.—Vesper Service Reverend Jones F. Hamilton, Pastor of the Trinity Episcopal Church, Hattiesburg, Miss.

Monday, May 24
10:00 a. m.— College Auditorium
5:00 p. m.— Garden Party For members of the May and August Graduating Classes Formal Gardens

Tuesday, May 25th
2:00 p. m.— Memorial Program In honor of the Twenty-fifth Anniversary of State Teachers College

Mississippi Southern College

1940 - 1962

Football star Andrew Webb was killed at Pearl Harbor on December 7, 1941.

February 1940, was full of irony for State Teachers College. It was a month of celebration and mourning, of triumph and near tragedy. On February 1, the Mississippi house of representatives voted 113–0 to change the school's name; a day later fire almost destroyed Mississippi Hall. The following week the state senate approved the name change, and STC became Mississippi Southern College; the same week, the institution's first president (also a member of that 1940 Senate) died. Paradox pursued the school throughout the year, even the decade. In June the institution awarded its first bachelor of arts degree; before the year ended, the Southern Association placed Mississippi Southern College on probation. In 1941 the football team recorded its first undefeated season; barely six months later MSC suspended intercollegiate athletics when the United States found itself, for the second time in a generation, embroiled in a profoundly destructive global war. This one almost destroyed the college. Enrollment, which had climbed from its Depression slump to a peak of 1500 in 1939, plunged by 1944 to a historic low. The male population almost disappeared entirely, as military service took from the campus, in the words of one professor, all but "4-F students

and theologues." Colleagues teasingly referred to the dean of students as the "dean of women." The faculty shrank to forty.

But what the exigencies of war removed with one hand they gave back with the other, producing by the end of the 1940s immense growth and prosperity for Mississippi Southern College. After the Japanese attack on Pearl Harbor, the war dominated campus life. A hastily organized civilian defense program reflected the mood of anxious uncertainty. Coach Thad Vann became air-raid warden for the college and outlined emergency procedures to the students during a solemn chapel session. "If the raid starts when you are away from home," he said, "lie down under shelter. . . . If an incendiary hits your house, go put it out with a spray (never a stream, jet, or splash) of water." Above all, Vann concluded, "Don't believe wild rumors. Don't crowd. Don't scream. Don't telephone. Don't start disorder or panic. Do what the Air-Raid Warden tells you to do. Be strong, be calm, be orderly. Lick the aggressors—everyone can help. Do your share!"

Fears of immediate danger soon gave way to grim but hopeful determination. In the fall of 1942, the U.S. War Department established an army ad-

ministration school on campus to train staff for military camps. The 165-member classes rotated through the eight-week school in staggered intervals with two classes on campus all the time, one entering and another leaving every four weeks. One occupied the stadium dormitory, and the other Forrest County Hall. The army also commandeered the second and third floors of College Hall for classrooms, several offices in the Administration Building, half the dining hall for mess, and the band hall for a quartermaster's building. The twenty-eight student occupants of the "Rock," as East Stadium was called, moved into the campus hospital under the supervision of nurse Beedie Smith, "Granny" to the campus community. "I lost 30 pounds and 11 months sleep the first year," she said, "but I wouldn't have missed it for anything in the world! We fussed, fought, and were friends together." When the army transferred its administration school to Fort Washington in January 1944, the college rented the East Stadium rooms to forty-nine families of men stationed at Camp Shelby, and soldiers continued to overrun the campus and the town until peace returned.

The war years also brought significant administrative changes, culminating in the appointment

73

World War II and its aftermath dominated college life throughout the forties. The drastic drop in enrollment, especially among men, created unique opportunities for females like star debater Evelyn Gandy, left, who later became Mississippi's first woman lieutenant governor. Thanks to nearby Camp Shelby and an army administration school on campus, soldiers became a familiar part of college life. A postwar resurgence in enrollment forced the construction of additional housing like McMillin and McCleskey Halls, shown here, opposite page, behind the partially completed West Stadium dormitory.

of a new president. Politics continued to plague higher education in Mississippi, despite the safeguards built into the new structure. Governors quickly learned to manipulate the new board almost as effectively as they had the old ones, simply by expanding its membership. The 1936 legislature added three new trustees, giving Governor Hugh White six appointees out of the board's twelve. Holding the tie-breaking ex-officio chairmanship himself, White restored control of the board to the governor's office. His successor, Paul Johnson, persuaded the lawmakers in 1940 that the board needed two additional members, a change that conveniently gave him eight appointments out of fourteen. By then many MSC faculty members openly referred to themselves as Conner, White, or Johnson appointees. And so it went.

When the college summarily dismissed three professors in the summer of 1940, the Southern Association again intervened to place the school on probation. Undoubtedly victims of a Johnson purge, Henry Ware, Truman Lewis, and B. F. Rivers were probably not so much egregious political offenders as they were simply the most expendable obstacles to the new governor's ability to pay political debts. Johnson needed jobs for his

R. C. Cook, below, became president in 1945 and made the renovated president's home, left, the centerpiece of a revitalized campus social life.

friends, and the positions held by these three must have seemed as good as any. Ware and Lewis had made themselves especially attractive targets by dabbling in interracial activities. Ware even helped organize a Mississippi affiliate of the Southern Commission on Interracial Cooperation, bringing to Hattiesburg an interracial educational institute that featured, among others, Mrs. Jessie Daniel Ames, founder of the Association of Southern Women for the Prevention of Lynching.

The 1942 legislature again tried to remove the colleges from the political spoils system by making the board a constitutional body. Voters in a November referendum approved an amendment to the state's fundamental law that reconstituted the board into a thirteen-member body whose structure and powers could be changed only by the same cumbersome and difficult amendment process. In December the Southern Association lifted MSC's probation.

In January 1945 the new board refused to reelect J. B. George as president of Mississippi Southern College. His downfall, according to Alma Hickman, was a result of "his inability to win the support of the students, faculty, and alumni." Yet

Homecoming parade on Main Street in downtown Hattiesburg.

however unpopular his restrictive policies had become, it was his steady administrative hand and sound fiscal management that preserved the institution through a savage depression and a wrenching war. The college owed him much.

H. M. Craft, who had replaced Lowrey as dean in 1941, ran the school until June, when the board named Robert Cecil Cook as the college's fourth president. Cook was still on active duty with the army education program in Europe and later claimed that he did not learn of his selection until he arrived in New York in July and a friend showed him the announcement in a Mississippi newspaper clipping. Immediately he reported to Camp Shelby where the army discharged him on July 6, his forty-second birthday. On the seventh, Cook paid his first ever visit to the campus where he found the president's home occupied by two faculty boarders and its back yard by the remnants of Dr. George's modest poultry farm. After Mrs. Cook evicted the tenants and cleaned out the chicken coops, the college renovated the thirty-three-year-old dwelling, which soon became the centerpiece of the new president's campaign to revitalize campus social life. The Cooks were, it seemed, always hosting various functions to entertain students, faculty, or alumni—as many as 5000 during one particularly busy year.

Cook held a bachelor's degree from Mississippi State College and both master's and doctoral degrees from Columbia University. He had been a teacher and superintendent in Mississippi's public schools and had served the University of Mississippi as principal of its Demonstration School, as well as associate professor and eventually dean of the school of education. His academic credentials were impeccable. But primarily R. C. Cook was a promoter, and he immediately set about promoting Mississippi Southern College. During that first campus visit, Dean Craft assembled an impromptu faculty meeting at which Cook predicted that enrollment would soon top 2000. His optimism both stunned and amused the fifty-one members of the faculty and staff, who at that moment were serving a student body of barely 300. They must have been more stunned, if not more amused, when enrollment quadrupled in two years and did reach 2000 by 1950.

Cook hoped to attract not just Mississippi students in general but particularly those from the Hattiesburg area. In those days, as one faculty member acknowledged, "local people, at least of society level, wouldn't think of sending their children out here . . . they would send them to Ole Miss or to the east." Many of them referred to Southern derisively as "Hardy Street High." Cook was determined to change that and spent much of his time and energy building bridges to the community; some on campus thought "he catered to the town too much." In any case, he hoped to increase Southern's appeal to a broad range of students by promoting excellence in three areas: academics, athletics, and social life. Progress had to begin, he believed, with a "program of superior instruction in a well organized and varied curriculum." The *Printz* reported that "his eagerness for . . . Southern's football future is as intense as the most ardent sportsman of Mississippi Southern College." And in a striking contrast to his predecessor, Cook was an ardent advocate of "good wholesome entertainment," including "dances, parties, and other social activities."

To accommodate the flood of returning veterans, the college rented unused apartment facilities at Camp Shelby, left, which became known as Veterans Village, and bought several white frame military surplus buildings, which by 1950 virtually dotted the entire campus, opposite page.

The 1946–47 session brought to campus a flood of veterans, who placed a huge strain on college housing. The school imported from Camp Shelby two prefabricated structures, one for married students (now McMillin Hall) and another for married faculty (now McCleskey Hall), and from the National Housing Agency, twenty-two trailer units which were placed opposite Faulkner Field. The temporary buildings, said Cook, would provide "adequate light-housekeeping quarters to the GIs who will of necessity have to bring their families with them—but who can't afford to pay high rent." For another 175 couples, the school secured access to a cluster of Camp Shelby apartments that soon became known as Veterans Village. Cook also purchased a fleet of buses to transport the students to the campus and back each day. The surge in enrollment strained more than just housing facilities. The fine arts division moved out of the crowded third floor of College Hall into a frame building that Cook also purchased from Camp Shelby and placed on the Demonstration School playground. Several other departments also held classes in temporary structures, most of which were "beastly hot," as one faculty member recalled. "It wasn't too

uncommon to see a professor under a tree with his students."

The large influx of veterans changed the entire nature of the college. For the first time, males made up a large percentage of the student population, and Cook felt that the curriculum "had to go in directions other than teaching." The Veterans Administration opened on campus a veterans' advisement center that provided education and vocational guidance, including complete counseling service and diagnostic tests, to former servicemen in a fifteen-county area around Hattiesburg. Business proved especially popular with veterans, and in 1946 business education and commerce, which had been a department within social studies, became a separate division. Joseph Green assumed the chairmanship in 1949 and over the next twenty years developed the program into today's highly respected College of Business Administration. Also in 1946 biology broke away from the physical sciences and mathematics to become an independent division under J. Fred Walker, who had been on the science faculty since 1926.

In 1947 the board allowed the establishment of a graduate program, making Mississippi Southern

College the third institution in the state to offer a master's degree in education. There were emphases in administration, secondary, elementary, and physical education, with both thesis and non-thesis options, each requiring forty-eight hours for graduation. To head the new graduate division, Cook appointed former dean of Mississippi College W. H. Sumrall. A 1948 state law authorized Mississippi Southern College "to make the training of teachers the principal object instead of the sole object . . . and to eliminate the provision that the course in such school shall always be confined to a strictly normal course for training teachers." The legislature also allowed the college to offer a bachelor of science degree without a professional teaching component.

The 1949–50 catalogue listed a B.S. curriculum that did not distinguish between teaching and non-teaching degrees. It included composition (ten hours), English literature (eight), speech (four), library science (one), social studies (fourteen), Mississippi history (four), science—biology, chemistry, and physics—(twelve), mathematics (four) science or mathematics elective (four), psychology (four), health and physical education (six). The addition of

a major and minor (professional courses for teachers) still left a total of 192 quarter hours for graduation. This served as the school's general curriculum for another twenty years. In 1954 Cook established the Basic College to administer the required curriculum, and for the next twenty years, all students spent their first two years enrolled in it. Also in the early fifties, MSC instituted the designations "honors" and "highest honors" for graduation. Another significant addition to the curriculum appeared in 1950 when R.O.T.C. came to campus.

Shortly after the war, Wilbur Stout, chairman of the Division of Language and Literature, established a four-year radio course in the speech department under Mary Tom Colones. Colones held a master's degree in radio and drama from the University of North Carolina where she had been a member of Professor Frederick Koch's famous Carolina Playmakers. Besides teaching courses in radio, she also assumed direction of major campus dramatic productions from long-time dramatic club sponsor Alma Hickman. With the cooperation of Hattiesburg station WFOR, the school constructed a fully-equipped studio under the north porch of Mississippi Hall, though it later moved to the third floor of College Hall. By 1951 the radio workshop

was producing shows on local stations, and two years later WMS, the college's own ten-watt station, went on the air.

Three new research and service centers emerged during Cook's presidency. In 1946 R. A. Pulliam organized the Reading Clinic, building on the work of Emily Jones, who had organized reading conferences for school teachers as early as the 1920s. The clinic, as part of the department of education and psychology, sought to educate teachers, clinicians, and researchers in the whole field of reading. Its diagnostic and treatment services for individual reading problems drew adults and children from throughout Mississippi and surrounding states and in 1953 became available to college students also.

In 1947 the school established a Latin American Institute (now the English Language Institute) to offer intensive language and culture courses designed to smooth the transition of a growing

In addition to such traditional classes as art and typewriting, MSC by the early fifties offered courses in military science and radio.

number of foreign students to American university life. When the institute's organizer, Colonel Melvin Nydegger, died suddenly in 1951, Dr. R. C. Reindorp became director. By that time the institute had become "a two-way street orienting Latin Americans to the American way of life and Americans to the Latin American way of life." In this way it fulfilled Dr. Cook's larger vision of improving "cultural ties and understanding between Latin America and the U.S."

The third service unit that Cook established was the Speech and Hearing Clinic, which opened in 1949, offering clinical therapy for speech disorders, training for student clinicians, and courses for classroom teachers. It also conducted training courses in other Mississippi communities and helped devise a speech curriculum for elementary and secondary schools.

The rapid expansion of Mississippi Southern College placed a premium upon good administrators, and Cook quickly determined that R. A. McLemore "was probably the best academic person on the faculty." When Dean Craft left the school in 1945, Cook appointed McLemore to replace him. "Dr. Mac," as the students knew him, had first come in 1938 to replace Bell Wiley as head

of the history department. Except for a brief period as interim president, he continued as dean until 1957. The first new faculty member that Cook hired was a young history teacher from Louisiana, John Gonzales. After more than four decades of service to the institution, he remained on the faculty in 1987 as William D. McCain Professor of History. Also during his first year, Cook brought to Southern several people he had known during his days at the University of Mississippi. Charles O. (Chuck) Smalling, a two-time all-American football player under Pop Warner at Stanford University, had been an assistant coach at Ole Miss. In December 1945, Cook named him financial secretary, a post he held until his retirement in 1976. In their early days in Oxford, the Cooks had shared a duplex with a young couple from Michigan, Leon and Ivah Wilber. "I knew Mrs. Wilber to be one of the finest women I had ever known," said Cook, and "Dr. Wilber was an excellent teacher," so he brought both to MSC, her as dean of women and him as professor of political science. In 1946 Lena Gough took over as dean of women, but Mrs. Wilber remained as assistant and served the school faithfully in various capacities for many years. Others who came to the school under Cook in-

cluded Carl McQuagge as principal of the Demonstration School (later dean of education and psychology); Jesse Gore as manager of the bookstore and Wimpy's; Dorothy Lenoir as the first director of placement; Reginald Switzer, who was a little all-American on the 1940 football squad, as dean of student welfare; Ralph Owings as head of educational administration (later dean of the graduate school); Porter Fortune as professor of history (later dean of the college, he went on to become chancellor of the University of Mississippi); Jack Moore as the first director of public relations; Powell Ogletree as executive secretary of the Alumni Association; and O. N. Darby, who replaced Mary Pulley as registrar.

One of Dr. Cook's major accomplishments, according to his successor, was in making Mississippi Southern College "socially acceptable." He worked diligently to break down the "Hardy High" image. Having seen Ole Miss attract "a great number of fine girls with national sororities," Cook made the expansion of Greek life at MSC a major objective. The three national women's groups already on campus—Delta Sigma Epsilon came in

Professors -- Absentminded and Otherwise

Every institution has its quota of eccentric characters and Southern has been no exception. Emily Jones, who taught education from 1913 until her retirement in 1953, established an exemplary model. Her driving exploits were particularly legendary, as typified by one notorious encounter with a local traffic gendarme at the corner of Main and Pine Streets downtown. As she approached the intersection with her arm extended to turn, the officious policeman politely advised, "Ma'am, I'm afraid you can't turn here," to which Miss Emily replied with equal but firm civility, "Oh yes, young man, if you'll just stand aside, I believe I can make it." On another occasion, not long after she had purchased her first automobile, Miss Jones placed a frantic call to campus security to report that she could not locate her new car and was afraid it had been stolen. After some routine detective work, the Hattiesburg police informed her that the car had been located downtown where, it turned out, she had parked it while shopping the previous day, forgotten about it, and from force of habit caught the bus back to campus.

Miss Jones's successor as campus eccentric was English professor Wilbur W. Stout, who came to Southern in 1945. "Doc," as almost everyone knew him, employed an exotic grading system that included circles, squares, and dots in addition to the standard letters, plusses, and minuses. One especially infamous symbol was a dot inside an oblong box, representing a coffin and meaning, "You're dead in this course." Also notorious were Professor Stout's theme topics which ran from the pedestrian—"What Happens On Moving Day" or "Friendship"—to the provocative—"Did You Ever Do a Stretch in a Mental institution" or "Don't Want It, Don't Need It, Couldn't Pay For It."

In 1945 R. A. McLemore, left, became dean of the college and John E. Gonzales, far left, joined the history faculty. Four years later Joseph Green, above, became chairman of business education and commerce. Gonzales and Green would serve the school well into the 1980s, the former as William D. McCain Professor History and the latter as dean of the college of business administration.

1940—were all educational sororities. Cook's secretary, Jane McInnis, had been a member of Chi Omega during her college days at the University of Alabama, and with her help, he lured this prestigious national social sorority to Southern in 1948. Kappa Delta came the following year, and Phi Mu in 1950. A year later former Mississippi first lady Corinne Johnson helped organize a Delta Delta Delta chapter, giving the school seven national sororities. Attracting Greek letter organizations for men to Southern proved more difficult, according to Cook, because "the national fraternities took a more standoffish look at schools which had formerly been teachers colleges." Several did come, however: Phi Kappa Tau, Kappa Alpha Order and Kappa Sigma in 1948; Alpha Tau Omega and Pi Kappa Alpha the following year; Sigma Phi Epsilon in 1953. An interfraternity council appeared in 1948.

For $31,000 Cook bought a two-story frame structure from Camp Shelby, moved it on campus near East Stadium, and made it available to the sororities as a Panhellenic Building, complete with meeting rooms, a large lounge, and a kitchen. In 1949 Alpha Tau Omega acquired the renovated college barn and turned it into the first fraternity

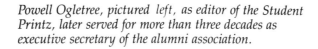

Powell Ogletree, pictured left, as editor of the Student Printz, later served for more than three decades as executive secretary of the alumni association.

house on campus. Five years later, Phi Kappa Tau broke ground for a building, and a fraternity row began to take shape at MSC. The development of fraternities and sororities during that period, Cook believed, "helped our situation from the standpoint of students better than any other."

Other kinds of organizations proliferated also. Besides the national leadership organizations, Omicron Delta Kappa and Phi Delta Rho, there were honorary societies in biology, drama, chemistry, commerce, education, mathematics, home economics, literature, music, foreign languages, religion, and speech. New denominational clubs appeared for Catholics, Episcopalians, Methodists, and Lutherans. Service organizations emerged, including the Pan American Student Association, Circle K, and the Yellowjackets, though the latter's primary service seemed to be hazing freshman. "Mississippi Southern," said Alma Hickman, "was becoming a big college in every way."

Occasionally, that came to include big problems. On a Wednesday evening in May 1952, a crowd of about 150 boys converged on one of the women's dorms in search of ladies' lingerie: a classic panty raid. Conveniently for the intrepid raiders, Cook was on a train somewhere between New York and Birmingham, returning from a meeting of the American Association of Colleges and the dean of men was in the hospital; no one was quite sure who was in charge of the campus. There had been some drinking, and "several of the students had physical difficulties," as Cook later put it, "with faculty members who tried to intervene." With the girls mostly urging the boys on, there was some minor scuffling, and someone broke down a door. Mostly, however, it was simply the delirium phase of spring fever, harmless, if not altogether innocent, fun. The president, however, according to Leon Wilber, "was very greatly distressed about it . . . afraid it would make a very bad impression around the state." He called a special chapel meeting on Friday morning. Not quite sure how he should begin, Cook suggested that it might be appropriate for the students to pray, so "they had

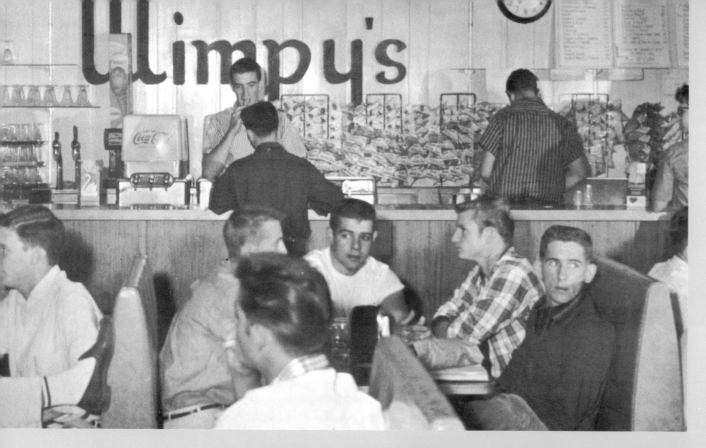

By the 1950s, despite a growing reputation as a suitcase college, above right, Southern could offer students a rich and varied campus life that ranged from the daring (panty raid, opposite page) to the frivolous (Sadie Hawkins dance, right).

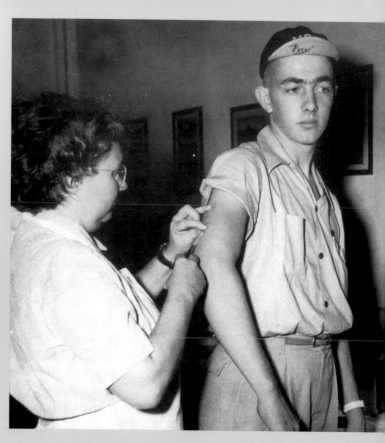

Under Raymond Mannoni, right, who became band director in 1952, the Pride and Dixie Darlings, opposite page, became nationally famous.

the Lord's Prayer," said Wilber. The president then delivered what he later described as "a most impassioned talk about honor and conduct." At the conclusion, honor gushed forth as 141 students voluntarily confessed that they had participated in the prank. More likely, it was fear that was gushing, because the president warned them that "names of participants were in the hands of the administration" already. After lunch the guilty gathered in the Administration Building to tell their stories to a discipline committee. Several were suspended or put on probation and the rest reprimanded. When asked what the administration would do concerning the "lingerie loss," Cook declared that the culprits would repay the cost "on a pro-rata basis."

Cook believed that in addition to a vibrant social life, a strong music program would enhance the college's reputation. "I realized when I came to Southern," he said, "that one of our best contributions (from the standpoint of state-wide recognition) might be in music," so he decided to "put a little extra money into it." Frank Marsh believed that an opera workshop might lure both more and better voice and string students into the music program. He decided to produce a complete opera, *The Bartered Bride*, in the winter quarter of 1948–49,

and hired as production director Lloyd Patten, who came officially to head the voice department. "None of us knew anything," recalled one of the cast, "the difference between upstage and downstage or how to use makeup." But with Patten's patient encouragement, "the Music Department . . . achieved a monumental event," demonstrating that a Mississippi college could produce a fine opera that could be enjoyed by a Mississippi audience. Other campus departments also contributed: a dance director (Laura May Hill) from physical education, sets from art and industrial arts, a lighting technician from English (Wilbur Stout), and publicity from the College News Bureau. Such collegiality was "a happy thing to see," said a local newspaper review, "in this compartmentalized life which we ordinarily feel obliged to lead," and the product was "a thing of elusive and enriching beauty." Except for a brief interruption because of the Korean War and the departure of Patten in 1951, the opera workshop productions became, under the direction of Leonard Stocker after 1952, a fixture of campus life. (The chorus for the 1953 production of *The Chocolate Soldier* included a young undergraduate from State Line, Aubrey K. Lucas.)

The marching band re-emerged after World War II but went through five directors in six years. Finally in 1952 Cook imported from Kansas a former University of Michigan assistant band director named Raymond Mannoni. "Before I knew it," the president recalled, "he had recruited over a hundred bandsmen and fifty drum majorettes." In a flash of marketing brilliance, the athletic director suggested that twirling females, if properly attired, might stimulate, among other things, a few extra ticket sales to football games. At Green's urging, therefore, Mannoni organized the Southern Belles, a precision dance troupe, to perform with the band. Now designated "the Pride of Mississippi" and armed with a stirring new rendition of Dixie, MSC's musicians soon became the official band of the annual Mobile Senior Bowl and remained so for three decades. In 1953 when a Montgomery, Alabama, reporter referred to the Belles as "those darlings from Dixie," another Southern tradition was born. "We had decided to have the only all-college dance-twirl group that we knew of at the time," said Mannoni. "Most of the corps used dancing only. Our girls were to dance, strut and twirl." The Dixie Darlings have since danced and strutted for almost thirty-five years, though they

The Madragallians entertain Governor Hugh White and other state officials, below, and Pride members admire new uniforms, left. Opposite page, trumpeter Spike Jones with friends, Porter Fortune and R. A. McLemore; and draft age fraternity brothers huddle around the radio to hear news of the war in Korea.

rarely twirl any more. Mannoni instituted two other annual events that fulfilled Cook's prescription for using music as a promotional instrument for the college. In the summer of 1953 the new band director organized a summer music camp that would become an annual affair, bringing to the campus high school musicians from throughout Mississippi and neighboring states. Many of the campers would later return as MSC students. In the fall of 1953 the school sponsored a band day during which nearby high school and junior high school bands performed with the Pride at a home football game. This, too, became an annual event and a valuable recruiting tool.

As the division of fine arts expanded, it began to outgrow its temporary frame quarters on the Demonstration School grounds. When Cook raised the question of a new fine arts building, Governor Hugh White scoffed at the chances of persuading a legislature highly sensitive to the needs of Delta planters and hill farms to open the floodgates of the treasury "for a group of fiddlers." Undaunted, Cook invited the lawmakers to a banquet at Jackson's Hotel Heidelberg, where MSC's orchestra, chorus, notable athletes, and others gave them "quite a show." Before the festivities ended, ac-

cording to Cook, the legislators were solidly committed to a $450,000 appropriation for the needed facility.

By the time Cook came to the college, the Lyceum course had long since disappeared, but the college continued to attract notable speakers and entertainers. The Trapp Family Singers and former Austrian Chancellor Kurt Schushnigg appeared on campus during the forties, and the Anglo-American poet W. H. Auden came in 1952. Two years later the students filled Bennett Auditorium twice, for Harry James in September and Spike Jones in October.

*A*thletics under R. C. Cook truly began to prosper at MSC, with football leading the way. Even before the war, Green and Vann had laid a firm foundation for the gridiron squad, which after 1940 bore the nickname Southerners—another of the era's ironies considering the contributions of a host of "Yankees" with names like Carazzo, Allesandri, Katrishen, Ovca, and Vetrano. After the 1940 season, the Detroit Lions made end Joe Stringfellow the school's first National Football League draftee. Mississippi Southern College carved its niche in

the football world in a fashion befitting the institution's heritage. Typical was the story of a young singlewing tailback named C. L. Dews, who came to Southern so small that Green was at first reluctant to play him, afraid he might be injured. Somehow by his junior year Dews added ten extra pounds, enough to overcome the anxiety of the coaches, who nicknamed him "Dipsey" and unleashed him on opponents whose defenses he riddled with his passing and running. In his final season Dews led the 1941 squad to nine victories and the school's first undefeated record, marred only by a scoreless tie with Southwestern Louisiana Institute.

The war ended football from 1942 to 1946, as both Green and Vann, along with most of the players, entered the military service. Again, however, the war gave with one hand what it had taken with the other. Out of the rental fee that the army paid for using the school facilities, President George set aside $25,000 to rebuild the athletic program after the war. Moreover, returning veterans swelled the pool of available athletes, leaving many prominent football schools with more players than they could use. When Vann and Green returned, they scoured the South for players willing to abandon

reserve status on noted teams for almost certain starting opportunities at MSC. To go with such transfers was an abundance of home-grown talent, including a running back known as "Bubber." John Melvin Phillips came to Hattiesburg in 1947 after scoring 235 points the previous year as a senior at Macon, Mississippi, High School. In his first college game against the University of Alabama, he scored six more. Trailing 13-0 in the third quarter, Southern halfback Bennie Ray Nobles took a pitch from quarterback Joe Romo and then lofted a pass to end "Spot" Honaker; Honaker in turn lateraled the ball to Phillips, who raced to the end zone to complete a remarkable 71-yard touchdown play. The Crimson Tide went on to crush MSC 34-7, but it would not be long before the ambitious Southerns would learn to hold their own against the likes of Alabama, and in much more conventional fashion. In its very next outing, the team upset Auburn 19-13 in Montgomery's Crampton Bowl and went on to a 7-3 record and the SIAA championship.

The following year MSC joined Spring Hill College of Mobile and seven Louisiana institutions to form the Gulf States Conference, whose football crown Southern promptly captured. That 1948 sea-

son was Green's last as head coach. The next year he became the school's first full-time athletic director, relinquishing the head coaching duties to Thad Vann. The Reed Green era gave to Southern fifty-four victories (twenty-one losses and four ties) and, in addition to those already mentioned, such memorable names as "Pel" Autry, "Tuffy" Johnson, "Hindu" Reynolds, Jay Smith, "Bucky" Waters, Maxie Lambright, Pete Taylor, "Ape" Snell, and "Apple" Sanders.

Pie Vann's initiation into the head coaching fraternity was rude in the extreme. It was administered by a colleague named Paul Bryant, whose Kentucky Wildcats, led by quarterback Babe Perelli, humiliated the Southerners 71-7. But Vann and his assistants, Clyde "Heifer" Stuart and H. A. Smith, regrouped their troops, who then reeled off six straight wins on their way to a 7-3 season, in which end Cliff Coggin set three national pass catching records. Nineteen fifty brought a second GSC crown and Coach of the Year honors to Vann, but the team barely broke even for the season. Though one of the five wins was over a University of Louisville team led by John Unitas, two of the five losses were embarrassing shutouts at the hands of Southeastern Conference powers Ten-

Opposite page, football stars "Bubber" Phillips, far left, and "Dipsey" Dews. Below, Leonard Williams' sensational catch sets up the winning touchdown against top-ranked Alabama in 1953.

nessee (56-0) and Alabama (53-0). The school won a third GSC championship in 1951 before withdrawing from the league the following year. Green hoped to turn Southern into a major competitor in college football, and independent status would, he thought, free him to add more prominent names to the schedule. Also in 1952, the school joined the National Collegiate Athletic Association, the major

But playing respectable teams was obviously not enough; the Southerners needed to defeat a national power to make a real mark. They came close in 1951, losing to LSU 13-0. Alabama, however, remained stubbornly invincible, thrashing MSC the same year 40-7. But Vann saw promise the next year, as his bruising defense forced the Crimson Tide into an SEC record twelve fumbles before finally bowing 20-6 to a team that would go on to crush Syracuse 61-6 in the Sugar Bowl. The 1952 squad finished 10-1, scoring fifty or more points four times and making the first bowl appearance in school history, a disappointing 26-7 loss to the College of the Pacific in El Paso's Sun Bowl.

The big break came in 1953. Southern opened the season against Alabama on September 18 in

Nick Revon, below, was the most prolific scorer in school history. His 2024 points led the basketball team to a host of victories, including the Sun Bowl Tournament championship in 1951, opposite page.

Montgomery. With Bart Starr at the helm, Red Drew's Tide was a consensus top-ten pick and Grantland Rice's choice to win the national championship. But behind the running of Hugh Laurin Pepper and Bucky McElroy, the passing of Billy Jarrell, and the sensational pass catching of Leonard Williams, Vann's squad stunned Alabama and the football world with a 25-19 upset that gave not only the football team but the institution instant identity from coast to coast. All the publicity was, however, a mixed blessing, as rumors emerged concerning the eligibility of Southern's athletes. In the face of charges that MSC was an "outlaw school," athletic director Green insisted that the program was "clean." President Cook instructed athletic committee chairman Lloyd Milam to collect all information available on the academic standing of every athlete at the school, and the committee kept detailed records thereafter.

The team won eight more times in 1953, including a 14-0 shutout of quarterback Zeke Bratkowski and Georgia's Bulldogs before 23,000 fans in Jackson. (Starr and Bratkowski would later quarterback the Green Bay Packers to victories in Super Bowls I and II.) A 27-13 loss to Memphis State was the only blemish on a record that earned the team its second straight Sun Bowl berth. The trip to El Paso again proved disappointing as Texas Western won handily, 37-14.

Lightning struck again in 1954, as MSC dumped Bart Starr and Alabama, 7-2. "Maybe some day," wrote Vincent Johnson of the *Mobile Press-Register,* "the Alabama schedule makers will get it through their thick heads that Southern is no jerkwater school that has to hunt around to find eleven men to fill up a team." In the *Atlanta Constitution* Furman Bisher suggested that "what Gettysburg is to Pennsylvania, what Appomattox Courthouse is to Virginia, what Ft. Sumter is to South Carolina, Crampton Bowl has now become to the football South." Heaping praise on Pie Vann, Bisher declared, "For two years in a row the man has managed to unzip the Southeastern Conference's pride and remove the stuffing." The victories over Alabama were more than football games. They, as much as anything else, established MSC as a major institution. Southern would never be considered a "jerkwater school" again.

It was also under R. C. Cook that the college established a respectable basketball program. Before 1949 basketball had been little more than something to occupy football players and coaches

during the winter, and Vann was the first football coach who did not also run the basketball team. When Texas Western graduate Lee Floyd became the first full-time basketball coach in 1949, the school also gave its first full scholarships in the sport.

Floyd "revolutionized basketball in Mississippi," according to sportswriter Jimmie McDowell. His "fast-breaking, hell-for-leather type play . . . caught on in rural and city high schools, in every hamlet, community, and town in the southern part of the Magnolia state." Starting four freshman in his initial season, he coached these "Cinderella Kids" to an 18-6 record and a GSC crown. His teams won twenty or more games in each of the next four seasons, giving him 117 wins (against 46 losses) during his first tour of duty (he would enter private business in 1954 but return to coach the University of Southern Mississippi in 1962). These included championships in the Sun Bowl (1951) and Senior Bowl (1954) Tournaments, two district NAIA championships, another GSC crown—and Coach of the Year honors for Floyd—(1951–52), and victories over Alabama, Texas Western, Memphis State, and New Mexico State. Southern fans, wrote McDowell, "will always remember the beginning—

the birth of Mississippi Southern's basketball team, and they'll remember the young Texas poppa. They'll remember the time Jumping Jack Gallagher tossed to Tom (Whiz) Bishop who zipped to Nick (The Cat) Revon in the finest fast-break of all, and they'll remember rebounding Mickey Harrington and battling Billy Allgood and velvet-smooth Jeep Clark. . . . And they'll remember big Mutt Watts and hawk-eyed Stormy Weathers and Jersey John O'Keefe's over-head shot for two points. . . . They'll remember all of Lee Floyd's boys because they were the pioneers, the products of the early good old days when Mississippi Southern was young and hungry."

Other sports also prospered in the post-war era. In 1947 the college fielded its first intercollegiate baseball team since 1930. The following year Vann took over the baseball squad from Green and coached them to the school's first win over the University of Mississippi in any sport. The 8-7 victory followed a heartbreaking loss the day before when the Rebels' Barney Poole (who would later serve as a football assistant under Pie Vann) belted a late-inning home run to secure a 2-1 Ole Miss win. Heifer Stuart replaced Vann in 1949 and would remain baseball coach until 1958. Several of

Vann's and Stuart's players went on to professional careers, including "Mel" Didier, Mickey Harrington, Hugh Laurin Pepper, Bubba Phillips, Fred Waters, and "Peanuts" Davenport, who also later managed the San Francisco Giants. By the 1950s the school also offered programs in tennis, golf, track, swimming, and boxing.

"So," said Cook, "with a very fine athletic program, a very fine program of music, . . . and with fraternities and sororities, we had the basis of what you might call student interest." The interest of the Board of Trustees was a different matter. There was a definite "pecking order" among the colleges, according to Cook, and Southern remained, with Delta State, far down the line behind Ole Miss, Mississippi State, and MSCW, especially when it came to appropriations. Securing money for salaries was always a struggle; getting funds for construction and equipment was more like a war. "Ole Miss and State would get two or three buildings," said Cook, "and then we would get whatever they had left." For an institution growing as rapidly as Southern, that became a serious problem, forcing

GO–
SOLID
FOR
SOUTHERN ✓

VOTE FOR X

the

MSC BOND ISSUE

on

Tuesday – May 18th

Why YOU Should Vote FOR X

the

Mississippi Southern College

BOND ISSUE

on

Tuesday, May 18th

A Forrest County bond issue, right, helped finance construction of the R. C. Cook College Union in 1956. In 1955 William D. McCain, opposite page, became the school's fifth president.

the administration to develop novel ways of creating space. Military surplus proved a godsend. In addition to the structures already mentioned, Cook, in 1949, purchased Camp Shelby's field house from the War Assets Commission. Thanks to the influence of Senator James O. Eastland and Congressman William Colmer, the school got the facility at the bargain basement price of $1927, an eighty percent discount from original construction costs. The State Building Commission provided $150,000 to dismantle, transport, and rebuild the structure at its present location near the southeast corner of Faulkner Field. The stadium itself grew in 1953, when a $350,000 appropriation allowed construction of a 5000-seat stadium dormitory on the west side. West Stadium also housed ninety-six male students.

Three new girls' dormitories further eased the campus housing crisis. Weathersby Hall went up in 1946, a dormitory for senior girls (now Hickman Hall) in 1951, and Bolton Hall in 1954. Other construction included a $115,000 expansion of the Home Economics Building (1947), renovation of the dining hall, which became a cafeteria (1948), a women's physical education building (1949), and the ROTC addition to the old laundry building

(1949). An annex added to the east end of Science Hall in the late 1940s had to be torn down in 1961 because of structural problems.

Two buildings were the fruit of extraordinary labors by Cook. One was a student union, which the president considered essential to his plans for a vibrant social life; the other was a student religious building. Unable to get the state to fund a student center, Cook decided to raise the money through private contributions. The Alumni Association voted in 1951 to sponsor the project, and Powell Ogletree and President Cook traveled the state soliciting funds from counties, towns, and religious groups, as well as alumni, faculty, students and friends. Within two years the drive elicited $200,000 in donations, and the state Building Commission added $50,000 for heat, light, and air conditioning systems. Barely halfway to the $450,000 needed, Cook then appealed to the Forrest County Board of Supervisors for the balance, noting that the new facility would provide lockers, restrooms, and a gathering place for local students. The supervisors agreed to call a special election, in which the voters overwhelmingly approved a $200,000 bond issue to support construction. Completed in 1956, the building became the R. C. Cook College

Union. When the new university union opened in 1976, the name was transferred to that facility and the old Cook Union became McLemore Hall.

The Danforth Chapel resulted from a fortunate visit to campus in 1953 by a representative of the Ralston-Purina Company of St. Louis. When Methodist student director Sam Barefield mentioned the school's need for a chapel, the visitor suggested approaching the president of his company, William H. Danforth, whose philanthropic efforts had helped fund college chapels throughout the country. Cook immediately chartered a plane to St. Louis where he persuaded Danforth to contribute $10,000 toward a Danforth Chapel at Southern. The Campus Student Christian Federation raised an additional $20,000 through blood drives, bazaars, and private donations, and the graduating classes of 1955 and 1956 left gifts totaling more than $1,000. The building opened in 1957, complete with furnishings that included a beautiful Thomas organ donated by Roseberry Piano House in honor of J. L. Roseberry.

In the fall of 1954, R. C. Cook stunned the college community by announcing that he was resigning effective December 31, to become vice-president and general manager of a new capital city

daily newspaper, the *Jackson State Times*. The offer of a three-year contract at $25,000 a year (he was making $12,000 at MSC) plus ten percent of the profits, a car, a fifty-dollar-per-week expense account, and membership in two exclusive Jackson clubs proved difficult to resist. Moreover, Cook explained, "I had just enough ink on my hands"—he had edited three nationally known biographical volumes including *Who's Who in American Education*—"to feel that I was capable. . . . it greatly attracted me." So Cook resigned at the end of 1954, the first president to vacate the post voluntarily. "I left Mississippi Southern College," he said, "with a very heavy heart." But his sadness could not have been greater than that of the friends he left behind. "The citizens of Hattiesburg just worshipped the man," one faculty member recalled, as did most of the campus community. "We did hate to see him leave so," said Anna Roberts, "we all cried when he left."

Indeed R. C. Cook's contribution to the school was inestimable. He transformed MSC into a modern institution. "He found it a small college," said Alma Hickman, "and he left it a much larger one . . . he greatly enlarged and improved the faculty and the academic standards." His decade of leadership left the "institution well on its way toward university status."

Toward that end, the selection of his replacement was, Cook later suggested, "almost providentially inspired." At the time, however, the former president, and others, probably believed that a less benign power had determined the choice, which then seemed more a result of conspiracy than inspiration. Whatever controversy Cook's departure lacked, the board more than made up for in naming his successor. First of all, they delayed a final decision for some time, naming McLemore acting president. Porter Fortune became acting dean. Meanwhile, Cook's venture into journalism turned into disaster. Not only was there ink on his hands, it seemed to be up to his neck; it was red ink, and he and the *State Times* were drowning in it. As the newspaper foundered, Cook began to explore the possibility of returning to his old job. By then campus sentiment had largely swung McLemore's way, and the former president's re-entry into the picture left the university community badly divided. It was, said McLemore, "a bad situation for both of us . . . many of the faculty people were supporting me, and some of the faculty people were supporting him; many of the alumni were supporting me and some were supporting him."

When the trustees met on May 19, 1955, they, too, were badly split. The board first voted on Cook and rejected his candidacy 6-5 with Chairman H. M. Ivy casting the crucial vote. A premature *Hattiesburg American* report that Cook would regain the presidency apparently angered Ivy, who already resented Cook's sudden departure for greener financial pastures. In an effort to unify all factions, the board then decided to go outside the university community and chose state archivist William D. McCain.

President McCain and his secretaries, Jessie Morrison (left, who eventually served three presidents) and Linda Grantham.

The college's fifth president was a native of Bellefontaine, Mississippi, and an early graduate of Delta State College. After earning a master's degree from the University of Mississippi in 1931 and a Ph.D. degree from Duke four years later, both in history, he taught at East Central and Copiah-Lincoln Junior Colleges, Ole Miss, Millsaps, and Mississippi State. In the 1930s, McCain served as assistant historian at the Morristown, New Jersey, National Historical Park and as assistant at the National Archives. He left Washington to become director of the Mississippi Department of Archives and History in 1938. Except for military service, he remained director until his selection as president of MSC. McCain began his military career in 1924 as a private in the Mississippi National Guard and ended it forty-three years later as a major general. In between were tours of active duty during World War II and the Korean conflict. In Europe he served in military intelligence and as archivist in Italy, where he supervised the collection and final disposition of more than eleven trainloads of material, including Mussolini's personal papers and numerous valuable works of art.

The Monday after the board's decision, which McCain described as a week of "bedlam," the pres-ident-elect scheduled a visit to the campus to address the student body. On Sunday night the students hanged H. M. Ivy in effigy, tossing a dummy of the board chairman from the porch of Hickman Hall into a flaming drum of gasoline, according to the *Printz*, "for his deciding negative vote" on Cook's bid to regain the presidency. "Dr. Cook did more to help Mississippi Southern than anyone else," one of the students declared. "Let's show the board that we disapprove of what they did to him." Student leaders insisted, however, that their sentiments were not against McCain, only the board's "mistreatment" of Cook. The next day McCain addressed more than 600 students, faculty, and staff who gathered around the east steps of the Administration Building to get a glimpse of the new president. They seemed favorably impressed. He mentioned few specifics other than his plans immediately to enlarge the library, winning him the undying devotion of Anna Roberts. Acknowledging the "great responsibility and challenge" of his new position, McCain concluded by predicting that MSC would soon be "a great university."

Back in McLemore's office, the acting president admonished his successor severely for using the word "university" in connection with Mississippi Southern College. McLemore advised McCain that he would get on much better with the board if he would avoid the issue of changing the status of the institution. The new president found out for himself two days later when he met with a committee of the board who informed him "in no uncertain terms," he later recalled, "that I was not to go to Hattiesburg and attempt to transform Mississippi Southern College into a university." The *Hattiesburg American* had several days before charged in an editorial that the board had rejected Cook precisely because of his success at MSC, that supporters of Ole Miss and Mississippi State were

*Bennett Auditorium in the 1950s, as seen from the
Administration Building.*

"afraid of what further progress Southern might make if he returned." If the trustees hoped that instructing McCain not to pursue university status would dissuade him from such a course, they were sorely deluded. "My father learned very early," McCain said, "that if he wanted me not to do something, it was wise not to say so, because then I might not think of it on my own."

The new president assumed his duties on August 18 and within a week recommended a reorganization of the curriculum. "There was no hope," he later wrote, "that Mississippi Southern College could ever achieve university status without first being given a university structure. I saw no reason to delay efforts in that direction." The proposal, based on a plan drafted during Cook's tenure, called for the establishment of three undergraduate schools—arts and sciences, education and psychology, and commerce and business administration—to go along with the existing graduate school. The board rejected it out of hand. McCain then decided to focus his energies on broadening and strengthening the graduate program. A year later he again proposed the reorganization but added a request for MSC to offer the master of arts degree in English, home economics, applied mu-

sic, mathematics, and social sciences. "The term 'social science,'" he said, "was used deliberately to confuse, for I intended for it to cover history, political science, sociology, geography, and various and sundry other subjects." He also asked for authority to grant the degree of doctor of education. The board referred all three recommendations to committee, effectively delaying any action on them.

McCain continued to push, formulating a third reorganization plan and maneuvering the March 1957 meeting of the board to the Southern campus. The board's education committee met for almost three hours on March 21, during which Chairman Reese D. McLendon asked McCain if he was trying to make MSC a university. "I stated truthfully," McCain said, "that the matter had never been discussed during our deliberations on reorganization and expansion." The board then authorized, on the recommendation of its education committee, Southern "to reorganize administration of instruction so as to provide for a Dean of the College and Graduate School of Education, a Dean of Arts and Sciences, a Dean of Education and Psychology, a Dean of Commerce and Business Administration." Fine arts and home economics continued as divisions. Each of these schools and divisions added

various degree requirements to its particular students' Basic College core curriculum—which remained that of 1949–50—after those students declared majors during the sophomore year. The trustees rejected the request for a doctoral program but approved non-teaching master's degrees in social studies, physical sciences, biology, English and literature, home economics, and music.

Without committing itself to the establishment of programs, the board allowed Southern in 1958 to apply, along with Ole Miss and Mississippi State, for federal fellowship money related to doctoral programs in education and marine sciences. Nothing developed from the fellowship application, but the next year, McCain asked the board to approve doctoral programs at MSC in education and marine sciences. "The second item," said McCain, "was thrown in for the purpose of giving the Board something to disapprove," which it did. But the college did receive permission to offer a doctoral degree in education with the provision that "requirements for admission and graduation be on a par [with] or better than those of previously authorized institutions." With the aid of the Alumni Association, McCain thereafter continued quietly but effectively "to educate the people of the

President McCain, pictured here with executive assistant Roger B. Johnson, vowed to keep the campus "dusty or muddy with construction" and, as he later concluded, "managed to do that for approximately twenty years."

state to the fact that it was inevitable that Mississippi Southern College would one day be a university."

Several other significant curriculum changes occurred during McCain's early years. In 1957 an Academic Council of elected faculty representatives replaced the old curriculum committee as the primary advisory body for undergraduate studies. Beginning the next year, all students had to pass an English proficiency test and all males had to pass six hours of military science to graduate. In 1961 the school again renumbered courses according to academic level: 100 courses being freshman, 200 sophomore, 300 junior, 400 senior, and 500 graduate.

Shortly after his arrival in Hattiesburg, McCain announced that he intended to keep the campus "dusty or muddy with construction." He kept that promise. One of the most pressing needs was for dormitory space, as the fall quarter's enrollment topped 3000, forcing the school to refund rent deposits to more than 500 students for whom no housing was available. "We must do something to take care of the Mississippi boys and girls who are clamoring to attend Southern," McCain declared. The federal government came to the rescue with

loans and matching grants that helped the school build five new housing facilities: two dormitories for women, Jones Hall (1959) and Pulley Hall (1962); two for men, Scott Hall (1959) and Bond Hall (1962); and Pinehaven Apartments for married students (1960). Several other buildings opened during McCain's first seven years: a new field house for athletics (1958), a new science building (1959, later named for J. Fred Walker), the new Cook Library (1960), the Commons (1962), and the Beedie Smith Infirmary (1962).

Several important personnel changes occurred also. In 1956 Roger B. Johnson became administrative assistant to the president. For two decades he remained McCain's right arm and was particularly instrumental in the acquisition and management of a flood of federal loans and grants that helped finance the president's building program. Gilbert Hartwig became chairman of the theater department, Joe Greene dean of commerce and business administration, Claude Fike dean of arts and sciences, Joel Eakins head of the physical plant, and Rader Grantham director of the college union (later dean of men). Porter Fortune replaced McLemore as dean of the college in 1957, and John Allen succeeded him in 1961.

The Walking Blueprint

Richard Gaines was a fireman, a plumber, a carpenter, and a general utility man. He was also a walking blueprint. He first came to campus in 1916 to visit a nephew who worked in the dining hall, and college secretary A. V Hays gave him a job firing the boiler. Forty-five years later he was still on the job, though state law required him to retire since he had reached his sixty-fifth birthday. But maintenance superintendent Harry Thomas applied for a year's deferment for him, pleading that "his knowledge of the underground utilities system, of which no record was made at the time of installation, makes it essential that he be retained until this information can be put on a map." It took several thousand dollars and a flock of engineers to design a map to replace the one in Rich's head. Finally on July 1, 1962, he was able to retire, but it took the maintenance crew a long time to break the habit of responding to crises by saying, "Go ask Rich."

There were also changes in student life. One of McCain's first acts was the abolition of chapel in 1955. Delta Sigma Epsilon merged with Delta Zeta in 1956, and a new sorority, Pi Beta Phi, appeared in 1960, as did another fraternity, Acacia. The college added honorary societies in economics, accounting, industrial arts, history, business education, band, speech, marketing, psychology, real estate, military science, physics, management, and drama. The reorganized Student Government Association included a Student Senate as well as Men's and Women's Affairs Boards.

The music program continued to flourish. In 1957 the music department sponsored its first annual Instrumental Conductor's Conference. Also in that year, Frances Jellinek became director of the Dixie Darlings, and the band introduced new uniforms, exact replicas of those of the Royal Scots Guards of Buckingham Palace, with red coats and black pants, trimmed in gold, and plaid Scotch tams. In the summer of 1960, the Pride and Dixie Darlings appeared before a national television audience during halftime of the annual College All-Star football game at Chicago's Soldier Field. The same year, Raymond Mannoni became dean of the division of fine arts, and in 1961 William J. Moody became director of bands.

Scene from Hey Daze, *left, a 1955 original musical production based on life at Southern. Basketball* coach *Fred Lewis, opposite page, compiled an 89-38 record from 1957 to 1962.*

As fellow teachers at a school in Alabama, Robert Hays and Richard Johnson had once dreamed of putting together a musical theater production. In 1955 they found themselves again colleagues, this time at MSC, Hays as assistant band director and Johnson as cultural relations advisor in the Latin American Institute. Their dream rekindled, they persuaded Mannoni to present the idea of an all-campus musical to the president, who appointed an interdepartmental Committee for the Coordination and Integration of School Spirit. The result was *Hey Daze,* a three-act musical based upon student life at MSC. Hays composed the show's eighteen tunes, and he, Johnson, Thomas Long, Patricia Hays, and Jacqueline Long collaborated on the book and lyrics. Carl Squitiero, a junior student from Bridgeport, Connecticut, wrote thirty-three pages of dialogue, and a Vicksburg senior, William Don Seay, did the choreography. Charles Ambrose of the art department designed and painted the sets; Wilbur Stout managed the lighting; Mannoni coordinated the general production. Recounting the adventures and misadventures of two student couples and a campus clown during a single academic year, the show featured familiar MSC scenes: Wimpy's, Faulkner

Field, classes, and the Dixie Darlings. It was, said the official program, an effort "to symbolize the spirit which has made Southern what it is today." Few people now recall Act III's grand finale, "Hail to the Black and Gold," but the song that concluded Act I has echoed at athletic contests for more than three decades; it was titled "Southern to the Top."

The *Hattiesburg American* called *Hey Daze* "a smash hit," and the company presented several more performances, including one in Biloxi and another in Jackson. There would be no more original productions after 1955, but Hays and Mannoni, with the help of Robert Treser and Gilbert Hartwig of the theater department and history professor John Gonzales, revived the all-school musical in 1958. That year's presentation of Lerner and Loewe's 1947 Broadway hit *Brigadoon* began a series of annual productions that included *Guys and Dolls* (1959), *Oklahoma* (1960), and *Damn Yankees* (1961). After 1961 the all-school musical disappeared as the division of fine arts and the theater department agreed that each needed to devote more energy to its own programs. Mannoni had assumed the chairmanship of fine arts in 1960, and the Southern Players had launched a summer stock

program the previous year. Fine arts continued to present musicals, however, including the summer band camp productions that began in 1960 with *H.M.S. Pinafore.*

*U*nder McCain the athletic program also continued to prosper. The 1955 football record was 9-1, followed by a 7-1-1 mark and a third bowl appearance—and a third loss, to West Texas State in Orlando's Tangerine Bowl—the following year. Vann's troops were able to do little better with the other half of the Lone Star State, losing to East Texas State 10-9 in a return trip to Orlando after an 8-2 season in 1957. The next year's team, however, posted the school's first perfect record, 9-0-0, and claimed the United Press International college division national championship. After 6-4 seasons in 1959 and 1960, an 8-1 mark in 1961 closed out the MSC era. Nineteen fifty-nine included a heartbreaking loss in Mobile's Ladd Stadium, where Southern outgained Texas A&M 368 yards to 195 but could muster only three points to match the Aggies' seven. The Southerners eased the pain somewhat with a 19-14 win over North Carolina

State later in the year, but the Wolfpack would repay the debt with interest, winning in 1960 and 1961 behind the strong arm of all-American quarterback Roman Gabriel.

Following Lee Floyd's departure, the basketball program lapsed into mediocrity until Green imported a New Yorker named Fred Lewis to coach the team in 1957. The new man brought with him a "run and gun" style and a new unofficial nickname, the "Golden Giants," which seemed more appropriate than "Southerners" for a lineup strewn with names like Goldberg, Lundberg, Grubar, Delia, and Migliazzo. With these players and others like Roy Danforth, Ken Fortenberry, Don Curry, Sam Hollingsworth, Robert Boothe, Harold Kea, Wayne Pulliam, and Clyde Mills, Lewis built a hardwood program whose success rivaled that of Vann's gridiron squads. In five seasons his teams won eighty-nine games while losing only thirty-

eight. The "Magnificent Seven" of 1960–61 finished 23-3 and second in UPI's college division poll. In another twist of irony, however, scandal struck just as MSC seemed poised on the brink of basketball greatness. In the summer of 1961 Hattiesburg police arrested three Golden Giant stars on seven counts of burglary. The players surrendered voluntarily and Lewis, who had cooperated in the investigation, insisted that they were not hardened criminals. But the incident was a bitter blow to the team, which slumped to 13-13 the following year, Lewis's worst and last at Southern.

*A*s the 1960s dawned, it was obvious that Mississippi Southern College was rapidly evolving into a major educational institution, one that would soon bid to become the state's largest. Enrollment was approaching 5000, and there were

more than 200 faculty and staff, many of whom held terminal degrees. But not everyone was ready to acknowledge the school's achievements. R. A. McLemore later recalled that "the most difficult job at Southern was to keep financial support adequate to take care of the increasing enrollment. [The legislature] couldn't believe the changes that were taking place. You couldn't convince the powers that there was this much development." But the institution's patriarchs had left a rich legacy in dealing with such obstacles. Half a century earlier a reluctant legislature had finally succumbed to the political potency of T. P. Scott's hand-cranked mimeograph machine. Seizing on that heritage, the generation of the sixties would again flex its political muscle to persuade the lawmakers to change the school's name to reflect its growth and progress. "Southern is a school of destiny," Reed Green had said amidst the football eligibility controversy in 1953, "and as we continue to grow rapidly it is only natural that others will label us as outlaws and try to ruin our prestige." But whatever the temporary setbacks, he concluded, "there is nothing that can stop Mississippi Southern from becoming 'the' school of Mississippi—both athletically and academically."

Alma Hickman, below, retired in 1954 after more than forty years on the faculty. At right, the campus as it appeared in 1961.

The Mississippi Southern College era ended as it had begun, in irony. The very year in which the institution became a multi-purpose university, 1962, also marked the golden anniversary of its origin as a tiny normal college devoted to the singular task of qualifying teachers for the rural schools of Mississippi. The moment could have been no more poignant for anyone than it was for Alma Hickman, who knew as no one else could have known what the school had been and what it had become. As poet and dramatist of the New Spirit of the Normal College, she had in 1919 prophesied of a future in which education would forever banish ignorance, which with its progeny—poverty, disease, and hate—had blighted so much of Mississippi's past. Though such an ultimate triumph remained as visionary in 1962 as it

had been in 1912, Alma Hickman had seen the institution that she helped establish wage a valiant war against the forces of ignorance, disease, and poverty. She could take comfort in the knowledge that so long as that institution remained faithful to its heritage, the battle would continue. As she reflected on Southern's evolution from a small normal school into a major university, she declared, "It is with great pride that I have watched this development from the beginning. I shall not, of course, live to see all of the future advancements of the school, but I can unequivocally state that I, as part of the small faculty and staff of 1912, take pride in viewing the realization of our dream and toil—superior education for the people of south Mississippi."

The University of
Southern Mississippi

1 9 6 2 -

Southern became a university at almost the precise moment that universities were seizing the attention of the nation. "The 1960s became," according to historian Paul Johnson, "the most explosive decade in the entire history of educational expansion." In modern culture's race, as H. G. Wells described it, "between education and catastrophe," the United States seemed determined to spare no expense to equip the former with every conceivable advantage, including the massive resources of a burgeoning federal government. Presiding over this idealistic war on ignorance was a former Texas schoolteacher who had worked his way to a college degree by sweeping the floors of "Old Main" at Southwest Texas State Teachers College, which had been until 1923—four years before young Lyndon Johnson entered it—San Marcos Normal. Four decades later President Lyndon Johnson announced to a confident America, "The answer for all our national problems comes in a single word. That word is education." Amid this general educational explosion, notes historian Johnson, "the growth in higher education was most marked," as the country became more and more wedded to the notion of a college degree as a universal right as well as a comprehensive good. In

the decade and a half after 1960, the number of American institutions of higher learning jumped by fifty percent while enrollment swelled to 9.4 million, an incredible 167% increase. By the mid-1970s the United States was spending $45 billion a year on higher education.

But American colleges exploded in another way during the 1960s. Four months after the Mississippi legislature gave the Hattiesburg institution its fourth name in fifty years, a group of dissident students in Michigan, led by Tom Hayden and Al Haber, drafted a manifesto for their newly reorganized Students for a Democratic Society. This Port Huron Statement, condemning racism, economic inequality, corporate power, and the cold war, became a blueprint for social change and the rallying cry for a generation of college students who made the term "campus unrest" a disturbing and exhilarating part of the American idiom.

Three months after the Port Huron meeting, and much closer to home, Southern's sister institution at Oxford exploded in violence when James Meredith became the first black to cross the color line in Mississippi's system of higher education. State authorities, after long and bitter resistance, finally succumbed to federal power and admitted him to

the University, but not before federal marshals and troops quelled a bloody riot that left two dead, scores injured, and Mississippi's public image badly tarnished.

The two events, the one in Michigan and the one in Mississippi, were not unrelated. Many of Hayden's ideas, as Garry Wills has observed, "grew out of [his] experience in the civil rights movement down South." Another veteran of the Student Nonviolent Coordinating Committee's Freedom Summer, Mario Savio, returned to the University of California in 1964 convinced that the same forces that repressed blacks in Mississippi also controlled Chancellor Clark Kerr's faceless, bureaucratic "multiversity" in Berkeley. As Hayden had put it, "Our professors and administrators sacrifice controversy to public relations, their curriculums change more slowly than the living events of the world . . . The accompanying 'let's pretend' theory of student extracurricular affairs . . . prepared the student for 'citizenship' through perpetual rehearsals and, usually, through emasculation of what creative spirit there is in the individual." Berkeley's Free Speech Movement challenged California authorities as SNCC had challenged Mississippi's. "Last summer I went to Mississippi to join the

At left, Governor Ross Barnett, flanked by President McCain and Lt. Governor Paul B. Johnson, Jr., signs legislation making Southern a university in 1962. Also present were (standing, from left) Alumni President Ralph McDaniels, Representative Stone D. Barefield, MSC Foundation President Moran M. Pope, Jr., Senator Frank Barber, Alumni Legislative Committee Chairman J. K. Tharpe, and Alumni Secretary Powell Ogletree.

In the mid-1960s registration was moved to Reed Green Coliseum to accommodate the growing number of students.

brief downturn in the late sixties, it began to inch steadily upward again, topping 10,000 in 1973 (main campus enrollment would not reach that figure until 1979).

McCain had to fulfill his "dust and mud" vow just to keep pace. The most pressing problem was housing, and five more dormitories went up before the decade ended: three for women, Wilber Panhellenic House (1963), Roberts Hall (1968), and Hillcrest (1964); and two for men, Elam Arms (1964) and Vann Hall (1967). Private interests built and owned Hillcrest and Elam in what the school administration hoped would be "a landmark in . . . future development," allowing the university "to concentrate its construction activities in the essential academic fields." Neither dormitory, however, proved profitable, and the school eventually acquired both, Elam in 1971 and Hillcrest two years later. A third private company owned Vann Athletic Dormitory and leased it to the university.

Other construction included the Education and Psychology Building (1964), Reed Green Coliseum (1965), Stout Lecture Hall (1966), a business administration building (1968, later named for Joseph A. Greene), the Johnson Science Tower (1970), the University Natatorium (1971, later named for

struggle there for civil rights," said Savio. "This fall I am engaged in another phase of the same struggle." In September 1964 Berkeley erupted as had Oxford two years earlier. Also by that time, the United States was discovering that what Hubert Humphrey once called "our great Asian adventure" was a morass from which every effort to disengage proved frustratingly futile. The Vietnamese tar baby offered student activists an issue fraught with the same kind of moral energy that evoked such passion in the crusade for racial justice. As the decade unfolded, the "student movement" spread across the country and etched a host of names and images on America's consciousness:

draft card burnings, Timothy Leary, Yippies, Bob Dylan, participatory democracy, Che Guevara, Woodstock, SDS, LSD, Hubert Marcuse, and counterculture.

Against this backdrop, Southern's entry into the elite fraternity of higher education sometimes seemed a mixed blessing. It was certainly a mixed blessing for William D. McCain, whose fourteen years as a university president were considerably more stormy and unpleasant than his early tenure at the helm of MSC. But USM shared as much, if not more, in the prosperity of the era as in its turmoil. Enrollment continued to grow, by almost a thousand a year from 1964 through 1967. After a

When the new Cook Library opened in 1961, the old facility became the Student Services Building, opposite page. The university rose garden, below, at the main entrance to campus was donated by the Hattiesburg Area Rose Society in 1973.

M. C. "Tuffy" Johnson), the Performing Arts Center (1972, later named for Raymond Mannoni), and the Nursing School Building (1975, later named for Elizabeth Harkins). Also during the sixties, there were major renovations of existing facilities: the Student Services Building (formerly Cook Library, 1961), the George Hurst Building (1964), College Hall (1966), and Southern Hall (1974). After the Commons opened, Wimpy's, the bookstore, and the post office moved into the remodeled Dining Hall, known as the Hub after 1963. A 1968 expansion doubled the size of Cook Library. The old Panhellenic House, renamed East Hall, became home to the departments of geography and religion and philosophy. A similar old Camp Shelby structure known as West Hall was torn down, though the theatre section was moved and renovated and opened in 1966 as the Southern Playhouse (later named for Gilbert Hartwig). Federal loans and grants continued to finance much of the construction boom.

After fire destroyed the Kappa Sigma and Pi Kappa Alpha fraternity houses in 1965, their replacements, along with a Sigma Alpha Epsilon house, inaugurated a new fraternity row just west of the old one in 1968. The Baptist Student Union,

the Wesley Foundation (Methodist), the Newman Club (Catholic), and the Southern Christian Student Center (Church of Christ) also built new facilities on or near the campus. In the late sixties, as growth cramped existing space, the school began to purchase additional property to the north and west of campus.

The attainment of university status inaugurated a period of rapid and extensive curriculum changes. The initial undergraduate structure included one college (arts and sciences), two schools (education and psychology and business administration), and two divisions (fine arts and home economics). Fine arts became a school in 1965 as did home economics three years later. In 1966 a special legislative appropriation enabled USM to organize a degree-granting school of nursing with Mary Elizabeth Harkins as its first dean. Education and psychology became a college in 1968.

The speech department was divided in 1964, with theatre moving to fine arts while public address joined journalism and radio and television to form a new department of communications in the college of arts and sciences. Five years later, the offices of public information, duplicating, printing, and photography united with the communications

In 1964 the university's program in radio and television, below, became part of a new department of communications. At right, theatre professor Gilbert Hartwig supervises the moving of the playhouse that now bears his name.

department in a new division of communications. Other new departments emerged during the 1960s: speech and hearing sciences, science education, and educational foundations in 1964; computer science and statistics (the first in the state) in 1965; and polymer science in 1969. In 1965 arts and sciences initiated an honors program (later the Honors College), which became university-wide after 1970. Other developments included: publication of *The Southern Quarterly* (1962) and the *Journal of Educational Research* (1968); establishment of a bureau of business research (1964), an office of research and projects (1964), and a computer center; and the inauguration of a free textbook service (1964).

In the summer of 1962 the university awarded its first doctoral degree in education. Thereafter, doctoral programs were added in biology, chemistry, political science, science education, music education, English and literature, history, mathematics, speech and hearing sciences, and geography. By 1972 USM offered terminal degrees in twenty-seven fields.

There were also personnel changes. Ralph Owings replaced Porter Fortune as dean of the graduate school and was succeeded in 1969 by

Charles Moorman. Anna Roberts retired in 1962 after thirty-seven years of service, and Warren Tracy became librarian. Sarah L. Weaver replaced Bertha Fritzsche in 1967 and became the first dean of home economics the following year. In 1969 Peter Durkee replaced Reginald Switzer as dean of student affairs. The same year, John Allen assumed the presidency of Centenary College in Louisiana, and Moorman became dean of the university. Registrar Aubrey Lucas became dean of the graduate school.

Moorman's inaugural address invoked a new concept, the career university, that soon brought sweeping and controversial changes to the curriculum. The new dean called for "a new dedication to teaching, a revitalized academic program, a sharpened awareness of public relations and service, and a renewed sense of academic community." Core requirements shrank from ninety-two to fifty-one hours, and the Basic College disappeared as new students enrolled directly in their major areas. A new five-day schedule of seventy-minute classes, adopted in 1972, allowed USM to award semester credit in most courses while retaining the quarter calendar. It also made a significant difference in appropriations after the college board began to al-

At left, Dean John Allen signs USM's first Ph.D. degree, which was awarded to Eugene M. Keebler in the summer of 1962. In 1965 Southern established a department of computer science and statistics, below, the first of its kind in Mississippi.

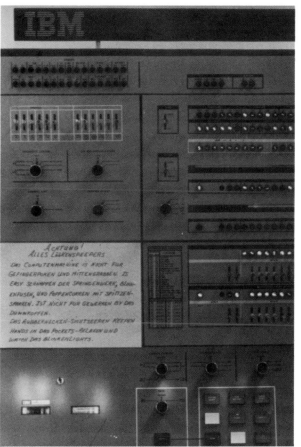

locate funds according to a formula based on credit-hour enrollment. The new schedule "was based on our discovery," McCain advised the board, "that in terms of class contact hours . . . we could quite easily give as much actual instruction per class in a quarter as do semester schools in a semester and . . . graduate our students in ten quarters instead of twelve, thus becoming the first true three-year university in the United States." Graduation now required 128 semester hours, 35 in the core and 18 in a minor, with the major determined by the appropriate school or college. The streamlined general curriculum included composition (6 hours), humanities and fine arts (9), social sciences (9), mathematics (3), science (6), and physical education (2).

Critics charged that the changes simply reflected an effort to conform to national trends in education and would lower academic standards. The word "relevant" did seem to appear frequently in defenses of the revised system, and many of the new programs such as American studies, Latin American studies, environmental studies, and black studies were similar to those established at other universities during that period. Other new programs also reflected the career orientation: athletic

administration and coaching, hotel and restaurant management, medical technology, linguistics, advertising, medical records, law enforcement, and plastics technology. Additional changes that were more or less related to the new scheme included new programs in dance, jazz, creative writing, aerospace studies, anthropology and comparative religious studies, recreation, microbiology, theater arts, and art education; an intermediate master of philosophy degree designed to serve junior college faculty; master's programs in criminal justice, nursing, and computer science; a new doctorate in performing musical arts; designation of health, physical education, and recreation as a school (1971); creation of a new graduate school of social work (1974); establishment of an oral history program (1970); and abolition of the English proficiency test and mandatory ROTC. A Career Development Center opened in 1974 to counsel students in choosing career programs. Perhaps the most significant aspect of the career concept was the separation of arts and sciences in 1970. Claude Fike remained dean of the College of Liberal Arts, and Robert van Aller became dean of the new College of Sciences, which three years later became the College of Science and Technology.

Discover USM

USM's refashioned "career" curriculum of the early 1970s featured a renewed emphasis on the sciences. Industrial technology student and New Jersey native Fred Cerami brought an exotic taste of Yankee enterprise to the career concept. His $300 investment in a hot dog wagon, below, launched a successful career in the restaurant business.

let's talk | the career university

SOUTHERN
THE UNIVERSITY OF SOUTHERN MISSISSIPPI

At left, Lena de Grummond, who established USM's renowned collection of children's literature, at the dedication of the Cook Library mural which Esphyr Slobodkina (left) painted for the collection in 1970. USM's speech and hearing clinic offered a variety of services to the community including audiometry tests, below.

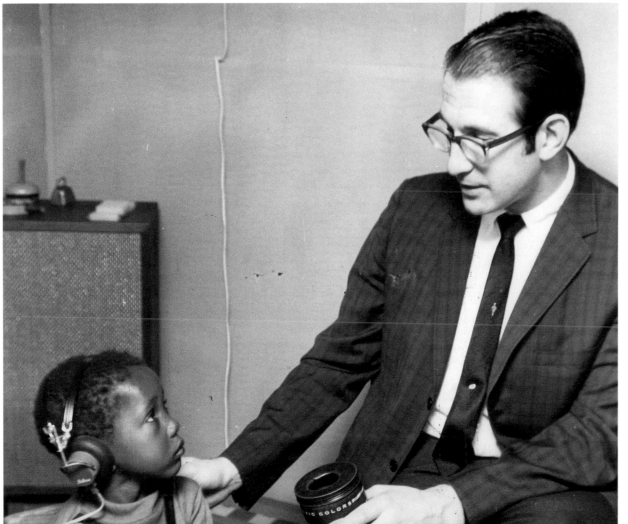

Despite criticisms of the new curriculum, Moorman defended the career university as "a great leap forward in education," one that made the academic program both stronger and more flexible. President McCain called it "another step in our forward march toward becoming the nation's most energetically progressive University. For we are now able to train our young people for active, useful, and profitable roles in society not only better than can more conservative . . . institutions, but faster as well."

The post-World War II enrollment surge finally spent itself by the late 1960s. On-campus registration declined in 1968 and 1969, the first consecutive decreases in a quarter of a century. The most popular explanation was the fading of the postwar baby boom which left a shrinking pool of high school graduates. Also, higher fees, especially out-of-state tuition, made competing institutions more attractive. The emergence of low-cost universities in New Orleans, Mobile, and Pensacola diminished Southern's yield from those traditionally fertile recruiting fields. Hurricane Camille's economic impact on Mississippi's Gulf Coast after 1969 constricted the student flow from that fruitful source also.

In the 1960s, USM expanded its services to "non-traditional" students such as Mrs. John L. Heiss, right, who earned a master's degree at the age of 91. The residence center in Natchez, below, became a degree-granting branch of the university in 1972.

In response to such trends, USM, like other universities, began to reevaluate its services to what became known in the 1970s as "nontraditional" students. Southern had begun, of course, as a service to an atypical college constituency—public school teachers—and had offered home study and correspondence courses since 1912. From 1954 to 1962, MSC sponsored an evening college "to serve adult members of the community" who wanted to "work toward a college degree, improve their occupational skills, study for self improvement, or pursue avocational interests." In 1961 the Division of Extension and Correspondence became the Division of Continuing Education (under Director Paul C. Morgan), which by 1969 included four departments: correspondence; conferences, institutes, and workshops; extension and residence centers; and community services. The last named began in 1962 as the Department of Adult Education, "designed to appeal to the professional, cultural, and recreational interests of the adult citizen of the University community."

Southern established its first residence center in Meridian in 1952 and a second in Biloxi in 1961. The following year a third opened in Natchez, pri-

marily in response to that community's appeal for an associate degree nursing program. The university also added permanent extension centers in Jackson (1964) and Jackson County (1972). In 1971 USM acquired the Long Beach facilities of Gulf Park College when that two-year private girls school closed after a half century of operation. The following year the residence centers at Natchez (under Dean Bill W. Gore) and Gulf Park (under Dean Joe E. Holloway) became degree-granting branches of the Hattiesburg campus, offering the bachelor of science in business administration, industrial technical education (Gulf Park only), and elementary and secondary education as well as courses in support of other degrees offered only through the main campus. Natchez continued its associate of science degree program in nursing. In 1973 these branches became part of a new division of extension and public service (under Dean Gomer Pound) that also included the departments of independent study, conferences and workshops, and community services and programs. The same year a committee of the Southern Association of Colleges and Secondary Schools visited the university as part of the decennial institutional self study. The

FUTURE HOME OF U.S.M. at NATCHEZ
COMPLETION DATE, FEB. 15

The Museum of Natural Science began in 1936 as a federal work relief project with STC science professors O. V. Austin, J. F. Walker, and John M. Frazier as advisors. Later named for Frazier and moved from Science Hall to the basement of Mississippi Hall, it became one of the most popular field trip sites for local school children.

committee noted that USM "appears committed to providing adult, continuing and extension education programs" based on the simple philosophy that "a modern university is under obligation to make its resources of knowledge, skills, and artistry readily accessible in consumable forms to all the community from which it receives support. The Division [of Extension and Public Service] seeks to thrust the resources of the University into the mainstream of the society it serves. By developing means through which the University can pervade all aspects of the human enterprise, the Division can thus enable the University to become a viable influence toward enhancing the quality of the lives of its constituency." In 1971 McCain informed the board that "through both credit and non-credit courses, the University increased the earning capacity and enriched the lives of scores of Mississippians. During the year our resident center enrollment increased 10%, our extension and in-service classes by 70%, our conferences and workshops by 70%, and our non-credit classes by an unbelievalbe 651%. It may well be that within a very few years, our off-campus population will be larger than that on campus." That prediction proved far too optimistic, but by the end of the decade, more than 2000 students, 20% of total enrollment, were taking courses away from the Hattiesburg campus.

In 1971 Aubrey Lucas accepted the presidency of Delta State University, and Robert van Aller replaced him as dean of the graduate school. Shelby F. Thames then became dean of the college of sciences. Also that year, Eric M. Gunn became dean of the college of education and psychology. The first dean of the new school of health, physical education, and recreation was William T. Schmidt, who was succeeded in 1974 by Walter Cooper. Sidney Weatherford became director of institutional research in 1972, and William Kirkpatrick replaced Forrest Tucker as director of public information the following year. Lester J. Glick became the first dean of the graduate school of social work in 1973.

The pulse of campus life during the sixties also reflected the dynamism of a developing university. The Greek community continued to thrive. Acacia disappeared early in the decade, but two new fraternities emerged: Sigma Alpha Epsilon in 1965 and Sigma Nu two years later. In 1969 another sorority, Delta Gamma, appeared. The prestigious scholastic honorary society Phi Kappa Phi came to the university in 1967, and the number of religious, service, and professional organizations mushroomed.

The music program remained one of the university's strongest. Alan Drake became director of bands in 1966 and was followed by Raymond G. Young in 1969, Joe Barry Mullins in 1973, James I. Nail in 1981, and Thomas Fraschillo in 1984. By 1975 there were, in addition to the marching, concert, and symphonic bands, a symphonic wind ensemble, chamber ensembles, a percussion choir and marimba ensemble, an ROTC band, and a jazz laboratory band. The University Singers appeared with the New Orleans Symphony Orchestra in 1964 and again in 1969. In 1967 the Summer Theatre, which had moved into the renovated Red Barn Theatre the previous year, merged with the

The USM Opera Theatre's 1974 production of "Die Fledermaus" was broadcast statewide by the Mississippi Educational Television Network.

Summer Musical Theatre to become the Southern Stage. Frank Monachino's production of *The Mikado* won a Mississippi Arts Council grant that financed a five-city tour of Mississippi in the fall of 1967. In 1970 Mannoni shifted the opera workshop from music to a new theatre arts department that encompassed all the performing arts including dance. The American Educational Theatre Association chose USM's production of *A Funny Thing Happened on the Way to the Forum*, directed by Blaine Quarnstrom, for a 1975 USO tour of American military bases in Greenland, Newfoundland, Labrador, and Iceland. In 1972 the new Raymond Mannoni Performing Arts Center opened with a production of *A Midsummer Night's Dream* that veteran *Jackson Daily News* critic Frank Hains called "the most striking technical achievement I have seen on a Mississippi stage." Two years later Robert Mesrobian directed USM's third production of *Die Fledermaus* in fifteen years, which became the first complete opera televised by the Mississippi Educational Television Network.

As a growing university, Southern was able to offer its students better and more varied entertainment. The Lettermen were annual favorites of the early sixties, and in 1965 Pete Fountain presented

the premiere concert in the new Reed Green Coliseum. Among the others to appear on campus were Bob Hope, Glen Campbell, Ray Charles, Chicago, Ike and Tina Turner, and the Temptations.

Lecturers included ABC newsman Peter Jennings, U.S. Senator and former astronaut John Glenn, former Supreme Court Justice Tom Clarke, and consumer advocate Ralph Nader.

Despite the turbulence of the sixties, college life remained, for most students, much as it had always been.

P. W. Underwood (left) brought to Pie Vann's coaching staff the same kind of aggressive defense he had exhibited as a player. Pep rallies were an exciting part of campus life each fall, especially when unexpected guests appeared, as did Mississippi State's mascot "Bully" in 1967, below.

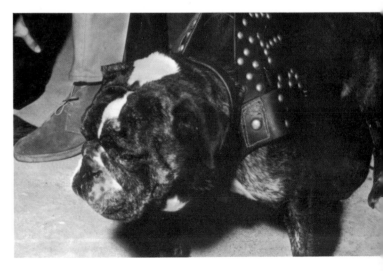

*A*thletics remained a vital part of student life. Pie Vann's 1962 football squad bade farewell to small college status by winning the school's second national championship in that division with a 9-1 season marred only by a loss to Memphis State. Vann's troops quickly established a reputation for gruesome defensive play that bore the distinct imprint of P. W. Underwood, who joined the staff in 1963. Behind a savage linebacking corps, which included Doug Satcher and Ken Avery, USM's "Vandals" led the nation in total defense in 1963, 1965, and 1966.

Despite carving a remarkable 39-13-1 record from 1962–1967, Vann found victories over Southeastern Conference foes frustratingly elusive, a problem aggravated by the return to the schedule of Mississippi State and Ole Miss in mid-decade. The renewal of the State series in 1964 was a 48-7 embarrassment. Quarterback Vic Purvis led the nation in rushing through much of the early season, which strangely included, because of scheduling problems, two games against Memphis State, both victories. The next year brought another loss to Mississippi State, though the SEC jinx which had lasted since the 1954 Alabama win finally ended against Auburn. The victory over the Tigers was one of three consecutive 3-0 games in 1965, the last of which unfortunately was a loss to William and Mary.

October 1966 was perhaps Pie Vann's most excruciating month as a head coach. After a painful 6-0 loss to Memphis State, he led his troops on a two-week foray into north Mississippi with high hopes of finally bringing down at least one of the state's traditional football powers. The invasion began ominously when Mississippi State's Marcus Rhoden took the opening kickoff and raced 95 yards to Southern's end zone. The 211 yards in penalties assessed against the two teams bore eloquent testimony to the brutality that marked the remaining 59 minutes and 37 seconds of the game. While the defense was holding the Bulldogs to just 85 yards from scrimmage for the day, Southern's offense clawed its way to a field goal and a touchdown in the second quarter, only to see a stray extra point allow State to escape with a 10-9 victory. The next Saturday's contest with Ole Miss, the first since 1939, began more auspiciously when USM turned a blocked punt into a first quarter touchdown. But with Dickie Dunaway punting 17 times in the game and Southern nursing a 7-0 lead into the final quarter, the kicking game eventually

Two of football's finest coaches and gentlemen, Pie Vann and John Vaught. Throughout the 1960s Vaught's Rebels remained frustratingly invulnerable to Southern's efforts to claim its initial victory in this bitter cross state rivalry.

reverted to previous form. Seventeen opportunities was too many to give the nation's leading punt returner, as Doug Cunningham demonstrated when he turned one into a game-tying touchdown. Less than four minutes later the Rebels scored again to hand Vann a crushing 14-7 loss, the second in eight days. The team rebounded to win four of its last five games for a 6-4 record and finally defeated Mississippi State 21-14 the next year. But it would be the dawn of a new decade before another October afternoon in Oxford would finally remove the bitter taste of 1966.

Unfortunately Pie Vann would not be there to enjoy it, for 1968 would be his last and only losing season. After winning three of its first four games, including a 47-14 thrashing of Mississippi State, Southern lost another heartbreaker in Oxford that seemed to demoralize Vann's squad. They dropped the next four games including a homecoming loss to Maxie Lambright's Louisiana Tech squad—quarterbacked by Terry Bradshaw—and a 68-7 humiliation at the hands of Don Coryell's San Diego State Aztecs led by Dennis Shaw and Fred Dryer. A victory over the University of Tampa in the season finale was not enough to erase the disappointment of a 4-6 record that, along with health

problems, led to Vann's retirement. His winning percentage over twenty years as head coach (70.2) ranks him among the nation's best, but his contribution went far beyond the 139 games his teams won. Whatever football success the University of Southern Mississippi would later achieve would be built upon the solid foundation he laid, as a coach and as a gentleman.

As the new coach, Reed Green chose former Ole Miss team captain and one-time Pie Vann assistant Roland Dale. When Dale, who had apparently accepted the job, changed his mind, Green turned to P. W. Underwood who had left Vann's staff in 1967 to coach linebackers at the University of Tennessee. Underwood got off to a rocky 5-5 start in his first campaign at USM, which included humiliations by Alabama (63-14) and Ole Miss (69-7). One of the few bright spots was a one-point victory over Louisiana Tech, the only blemish on the senior season of Terry Bradshaw, who would soon be the first player chosen in the 1970 National Football League draft.

Nineteen seventy's disappointing 5-6 season ironically would produce three major contributions to Southern's struggle to become a major football power. One was a lanky defensive back and kicking specialist from Thomson, Georgia, who celebrated his debut as a college punter by fumbling his first snap from center. It was one of the few mistakes young Raymond Guy ever made in a Southern uniform. That night against Southwestern Louisiana, he went on to kick three field goals and an extra point and intercept a pass to lead USM to a 16-14 win. But it was neither his placekicking nor his defensive play that riveted the attention of the sportswriters, as well as everyone else in Lafayette that night. During the fourth quarter, on fourth down at the USM 23 yard line, Guy again dropped back to punt. Standing on his own 9 yard line—this time he fielded the snap cleanly—he launched a prodigious spiral that ultimately came to rest six yards deep in the USL end zone. Officially, it was a school record 77 yards, but it rolled dead 97 yards from where he stood. The greatest punter in the history of college football had declared himself over the sophomore jitters, finishing the night with a 49.8-yard average on 7 punts.

The second notable feature of the 1970 season was a 5'4", 145 lb. bolt of lightning from Purvis named Willie Heidelburg. He was not the greatest running back in USM history, though he was among the fastest. His chief contribution actually had nothing to do with athletic skill at all; he was the school's first black football player, and his courage and affability helped make USM's transition to an integrated athletic program exemplary.

And these two, the rangy white boy with the cannon leg and the diminutive but fleet black, had much to do with the third great achievement of 1970. That occurred at Oxford on October 17, when John Vaught's nationally ranked (fourth by the Associated Press, fifth by United Press International) Ole Miss Rebels christened Hemingway Stadium's new artificial playing surface against USM. Fresh from back-to-back wins over Alabama (48-23, before a prime time national television audience) and Georgia (31-21), Archie Manning was seeking his third consecutive Southeastern back-of-the-week honors on his way to the Heisman Trophy. The sports pundits predicted, not the score, but how long the brilliant redhead from Drew would get to shine before yielding to his understudy to prevent a massacre more unseemly than the previous year's 62-point rout.

But well into the second half, Manning found himself still very much in demand thanks to two 11-yard touchdown scampers by Heidelburg and a

Southerners Fire The Shot Heard 'Round Football's World

By BOBBY HALL
Staff Writer

OXFORD, Miss. — A night's sleep has done nothing to alter the verdict and that same shocking score you undoubtedly have already heard by now still stands: University of Southern Mississippi 30, Ole Miss 14.

They are still celebrating this morning in Hattiesburg, home of the Southerners, and the tear-stained pillows in Rebel Land already have been hung out to dry.

But the fact remains that the biggest football upset since who knows when was recorded here yesterday afternoon in full view of 27,200 spectators, most of whom had expected to see the fourth-ranked Rebels toy with the unheralded Southerners.

That was hardly the case as Southern, which had never beaten Ole Miss in 10 tries, ground the blue-shirted Rebels into the plush green surface of their brand new Astroturf.

"Don't you say it's no upset," bellowed a hoarse Coach P. W. 'Bear' Underwood as he waded through a sea of enthusiasm. "We took it to their butt and we whipped their butt."

John Vaught, the Ole Miss coach, agreed, but didn't offer quite as vivid a description as the plump Underwood, who celebrated his 39th birthday Friday.

"They played an enthusiastic and inspirational football game," Vaught said. "They beat us in every phase of the game."

It all started simply enough. Ole Miss breezed 61 yards in five plays the first time it had the football to take a 7-0 lead. The decisive play was a 51-yard pass from quarterback Archie Manning to split end Floyd Franks. Jim Poole kicked his first of two extra points and only the Southerners had any idea that the Rebels were not on their way.

But late in the first period Southern's Bill Foley, a sophomore, stole a Rebel handoff at the Ole Miss 44 and blazed down the left sideline to score. Ray Guy, another Southern sophomore, kicked his first of three extra points for a 7-7 tie.

Still the Rebels weren't convinced the Southerners had come to play. Manning, using his passing arm frequently, guided the Rebels 82 yards in 12 plays for a 14-7 edge with 52 seconds left in the first quarter. The touchdown came on a 22-yard toss to tailback Randy Reed.

It all seemed so easy.

Then the Southerners erupted with a defense of iron and an offense with enough punch to battle the confused Rebel defense. Midway in the second period, Southern quarterback Rick Donegan broke away for a 46-yard gainer to the Rebel 19. Four plays later sophomore Willie Heidelburg, a 5-6, 147-pound package of dynamite, skirted right end with a spurt of speed for the typing touchdown. The play, which had not been used previously by Southern, covered 11 yards.

"It was an option reverse," said Vaught. "We hadn't expected to see that one."

Southern took the lead to stay with 3:19 left in the second period on a 47-yard field goal by Guy, whose kicking and punting were sensational all afternoon. He punted 10 times for a 48.6-yard average.

The Southerners, who are now 4-2 on the season, next play Mississippi State at Starkville. Ole Miss, now 4-1 and a loser for the first time in 10 games, will travel to Vanderbilt Saturday.

Before the Rebels had full time to realize that they were on the short end of a 17-14 halftime score, the Southerners struck again, using the same reverse with Heidelburg, one of two black players on the Southern squad, supplying the key yardage.

This time the Southerners marched 51 yards in six plays. Donegan passed for 11 yards to Marshall Veale for one first down, handed off to tailback Bob Moulton for 15 yards and another first down, then slipped the ball to the lightning-quick Heidelburg for the final 11 yards and a 23-14 edge.

"Nothing else any better can happen to us," said a jubilant Heidelburg, who was a star last year at Pearl River Junior College.

But it did.

With 5:45 left in the third period, sophomore Gerry Saggus accepted an Ole Miss punt at his own 40 and raced 60 yards through the broken heart of the Rebel defense for six points. Guy's kick supplied the final margin of 30-14.

From that point on it was the gutty Southern defense which stalled every Rebel bid. Manning took the Rebs to the Southern one-yard line once before running into an unyielding defensive end named Hugh Eggersman. The 205-pound sophomore stopped Manning on a fourth-and-goal-to-go burst with 36 seconds left in the third period.

Manning again took the Rebels to within sniffing distance of a touchdown. But sideback Craig Logan, who earlier intercepted a Manning pass, picked off another at the 11 to halt the attacks early in the fourth period.

"I'm really embarrassed," said Manning, who hit on 30 of 56 passes for 341 yards and two touchdowns. "I've never been beaten on that much. When those guys hit you they hit you good."

Manning figured in 69 plays offensively, a new Southeastern Conference record for total plays. John Reaves of Florida had 68 plays against Auburn last year. Manning's 56 passing attempts set a school record, breaking his own mark of 52 last year against Alabama.

"Now it's just a test to see what we're made of," Manning said in picking up the pieces of defeat. "There are only two ways to go: Straight to the bottom or back up. It's just a shame this had to happen."

But down at Hattiesburg it's a different story. The Southerners have just completed their grandest football hour. Yesterday afternoon the University of Southern Mississippi knocked over the giant of Mississippi football.

(Additional Story and Picture on Page 1, Sec. 3)

Ray Guy's kicking, above, Willie Heidelburg's running, far right, and Hugh Eggersman's (96) goal line stop of Archie Manning, right, helped seal USM's upset victory over Ole Miss in 1970.

1970
USM - 30   OLE MISS - 14
P. W. UNDERWOOD
UPI Coach of the Week

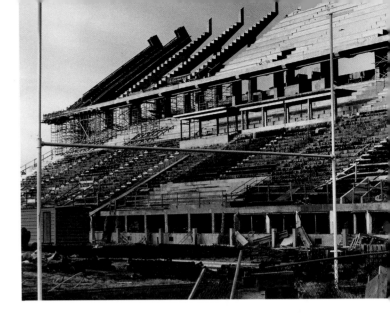

47-yard Guy field goal that helped put Ole Miss on the short end of a 30-14 score. As the third quarter drew to a close, Manning drove his team to a first down at the USM 4-yard line. Three plays later, on fourth down at the one, defensive end Hugh Eggersmen sliced through the Rebel forward wall, pinned Manning high on his shoulder pads, and dumped him, along with hopes for a national championship and the Heisman Trophy, onto the plush green astroturf floor. "Don't you call it no upset," growled a proud Underwood to sportswriters after the game, "we took it to their butt and we whipped their butt." But it *was* an upset, perhaps the biggest in either school's history, and it unfortunately overshadowed a magnificent performance by Manning, who completeed 30 of 56 passes for 341 yards and 2 touchdowns in the game. Possibly the greatest college quarterback of all time, he was as manly and courageous in defeat as he had ever been skillful in victory. Refusing to make excuses for the bitter loss, he paid gallant tribute to the foes who had so rudely snatched from him and his teammates an opportunity to reach the pinnacle of college football. "I've never been beat on that much," he told reporters. "When those guys hit you, they hit you good." For all that

this day meant to friends of USM, they would have to share its glory with the one whose nobility in defeat helped make victory mean so much.

And it meant a great deal indeed. The triumphs of the 1950s, ironically, had vindicated Southern's credentials everywhere but Mississippi. This win earned for USM within the Magnolia State what the 1953 victory over Alabama had earned elsewhere, instant respectability, and not just as a football team but as a university. By defeating, not any Ole Miss team, but this particular Ole Miss team, Southern served notice that it was no longer the state's institutional stepchild but was moving forward to stake its claim to the family football inheritance.

Brutal reality, wearing maroon and white, ended the celebration in short order, as Mississippi State unloaded two years worth of revenge in a 51-15 drubbing the next week. The team went on to suffer through the school's second losing season in three years, and Underwood was yet to finish above .500. His third campaign began little better, as the first six games in 1971 produced only a single win over San Diego State and quarterback Brian Sipe. But Southern won all of the remaining five games to give Underwood that elusive first

winning season at 6-5.

The prosperity was short-lived, however, as 1972 turned into a 3-7-1 disaster. A late-season game against Utah State symbolized the year's futility. In a blinding snowstorm, Guy kicked a school-record 61 yard field goal, only to have the Aggies block a punt on the game's final play and recover the ball in the end zone to win 27-21. Though the record got better over the next two years (6-4-1 and 6-5), the frustrations seemed to grow worse, especially against Ole Miss, who thrashed USM 41-0 in 1973 and the next year converted a fourth down play with twenty-two yards to go on their way to a last-second, 20-14 victory. At the end of the 1974 campaign, during which stadium renovation required the team to play all eleven games on the road, Underwood resigned. "After a great deal of prayerful thought," he said, such action seemed "in the best interest of my family and the University." Ironically, his last game, like Vann's, was an upset win over the University of Tampa. Affirming his pride in the progress of the football program under his direction, he declared, "I trust that my contributions will mean something in the future and will not be judged by the scoreboard alone." And one must indeed look beyond the scoreboard to see

In 1975 Roland Dale, opposite page, replaced the retiring Reed Green as athletic director, and Bobby Collins, left, became the new Eagle football coach. Renovation of the stadium sent the football team on the road for all of its games in 1974 and 1975.

how much progress USM football really made under P. W. Underwood. He gave the school a consensus all-American and its first NFL top-round draft choice in Ray Guy. Underwood had an infectious and enthusiastic devotion to the institution that helped create Big Gold Country, a phrase and an idea that he brought with him from Tennessee. It was under him in 1972 that the athletic program boldly defined a distinct identity for the university by adopting a new nickname, Golden Eagles. He helped dissolve the color barrier in respectable fashion, and he held the program together during the difficult time of transition that always follows a living legend like Pie Vann. And even if some choose to judge him by the score-

board after all, it will probably be the one that reads USM 30, Ole Miss 14.

The task of finding someone to fill Underwood's position fell to the man who had almost held it in the first place, Roland Dale. In December 1973, McCain had named Dale to replace Reed Green, who announced that he would retire at the end of 1974 after almost half a century of service to USM athletics. The new athletic director came from Southeastern Louisiana University, where he had been head coach since 1972 after spending time as assistant coach at Ole Miss and Tulane in addition to three years on Pie Vann's staff.

The search for Underwood's successor took only three weeks and ended with the hiring of University of North Carolina assistant, Bobby Collins. A Laurel native, Collins had lettered four years at Mississippi State, where he was an outstanding quarterback and punter. After graduating in 1955, he was an assistant at Mississippi State, Colorado State, George Washington, and Virginia Tech before former Bulldog teammate Bill Dooley brought him to Chapel Hill. He had served there eight years, five as offensive coordinator and three as assistant head coach in charge of defense, when Dale selected him as USM's head coach. Thus, a

new phase of Golden Eagle football began under the leadership of an athletic director who had been team captain at one cross-state rival and a coach who had been captain at the other.

The basketball program entered the university era under a familiar face, Lee Floyd, who returned as head coach in 1962. His second stint at Southern proved less successful than the first, and his 1962–63 team's 12-14 record gave him his first losing season. Despite two more losing campaigns (1965–66 and 1970–71), to go with six winning ones, Floyd gave USM another flood of memorable events—wins over Mississippi State (1963), Alabama (1966), and Ole Miss (1966); the opening of Reed Green Coliseum (December 6, 1965 against Southwestern Louisiana); a 23-game home winning streak (1966–69)—and players: Jackie Laird, Bruce Miller, Charlie Payne, Gary Kochersperger, Gary Hannan, Rich Corsetto, and Wilbert Jordan (USM's first black basketball player).

Undoubtedly the most memorable player was a 6'5" mountain of a forward who came to USM in 1966 from Necaise Crossing, where he had been one of the most intensely recruited high school players in America. Wendell Ladner left Hattiesburg four years later with school records for

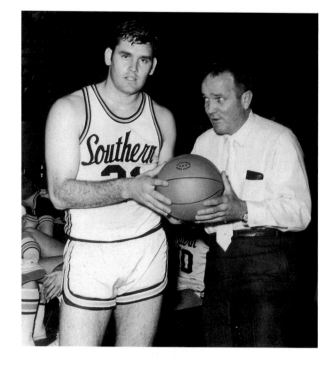

At right, basketball standout Wendell Ladner and Coach Lee Floyd. Pete Taylor, below, coached USM baseball for almost three decades, 1958–1985.

career average in scoring (20.5 per game) and rebounding (an incredible 16.5 per game). His 32 rebounds against Pan American University in 1970, 436 during the 1969–70 season, and career total of 1256 are also school records. He ranks fifth in career scoring with 1564 points. Ladner went on to a successful career in professional basketball before a tragic airline crash took his life in 1975.

Perhaps the most memorable season was 1967–68, when Floyd's team averaged 97.6 points per game and topped the century mark ten times on their way to a 19-6 record. Ladner's 21.4 points per game led the way, and John Vitrano's 57.9% shooting average set a school record (broken by Joe Dawson in 1979–80). Berlin Ladner entered the season finale against Samford only 39 points short of the 1000-point club, and teammates spent much of the night helping him reach that milestone. With "little" brother Wendell sweeping the offensive board and shoveling the ball back out to him, Berlin led the team to a 109-90 rout with a school record 45-point performance.

With his health declining and the team sinking to a 7-19 record, Floyd retired after the 1970–71 season. His 128-100 record after 1962 gave him an overall mark of 246-147. Eugene "Jeep" Clark, who had been Floyd's assistant since 1964, succeeded him as head coach. Clark's first campaign was an 0-24 disaster from which he would never really recover. After an 8-16 record the next year, followed by three consecutive 11-15 seasons, he resigned in 1976. Highlights of Clark's tenure included wins over Ole Miss, Georgia Tech, Southern Methodist, Rice, Lamar, and City College of New York and the play of Glenn Masson, Casey Price, Danny Thornsberry, and John Prince.

Baseball remained largely a non-scholarship sport, yet C. J. "Pete" Taylor, who replaced Clyde Stuart as coach in 1958, produced several outstanding teams. The 1964–65 squad finished 15-4 and defeated Mississippi State, Ole Miss, Alabama, and Arkansas. Memorable players included Frank Baker, Bruce Miller, Gary Hannan, Jimbo Green, Ed Assaf, John Flynt, and Wilson Plunkett.

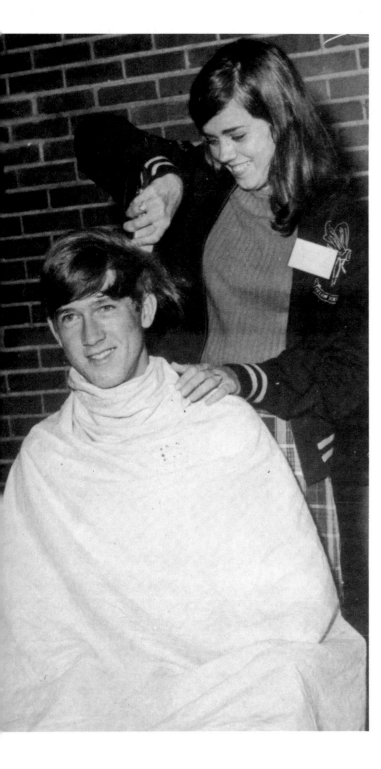

Freshman hazing, left, ended in 1968. Elsie Granberry's quest for name recognition, below, added a new dimension to campus politics in 1966.

*W*hile the college experience of most USM students remained much like that of earlier generations, campus life in Hattiesburg was not impervious to the sweeping changes that the sixties loosed upon American society. The first incursion by revolutionary forces came in 1965 when black students enrolled at the school for the first time. Others had tried before and failed. One, a young army veteran named Clyde Kennard, left a tragic and controversial legacy. Kennard, who had returned to his family's farm near Eatonville in 1955, tried unsuccessfully to enroll at MSC four years later. After a visit to campus on September 19, 1959, he was arrested for possession of whiskey (Mississippi was legally dry until 1966) and convicted in a justice of the peace court two weeks later. The following year he was again arrested, this time for allegedly stealing five sacks of chicken feed. Again he was convicted, in what civil rights activist and soon-to-be-martyr Medgar Evers called a "mockery to judicial justice." Sentenced to seven years in the state penitentiary, Kennard died of leukemia at Parchman in 1963.

After the Meredith incident at Ole Miss, McCain apparently realized that integration must come to USM, and he was determined that it come peace-

During the 1960s, students chafed at social restrictions, such as signing-out requirements and curfew for dormitory women. Some protested, as in the infamous "riots" of 1967, below left. Others, left, simply did the best they could under the circumstances.

fully. On September 6, 1965, the following letter from the president to the students, faculty, and staff appeared in the *Student Printz:*

Ladies and Gentlemen:

Two Negro students have been admitted to this institution. These students will be participating in the various orientation activities on campus beginning Monday, September 6, 1965.

It is expected that all personnel connected with the University will go about their affairs in a "business as usual" manner. We are certain that the fine conduct and spirit of our people will manifest itself during these times of change and that the University community will continue to show that we are "the biggest and the best."

And so segregation ended at the university without incident.

McCain was not so fortunate with USM's introduction to "student unrest" in 1967. Superficially, it began with all the trappings of a typical pre-final examination fling. Shortly after midnight on May 10, residents of Bond and Scott Halls began to congregate in the parking lot that separated the two men's dormitories. Their enthusiasm and courage grew with their ranks, which quickly reached several hundred. Finally someone uttered

the catalytic phrase, "panty raid," and the crowd jubilantly struck out for Mississippi Hall. Before reaching the target, however, they encountered dean of men Rader Grantham and security chief Willie Oubre at the head of a campus force now supported by several Hattiesburg police units complete with riot dogs. The mob splintered into smaller contingents that ventured off to perpetrate individual pranks. One substantial group re-formed in front of Panhellenic dormitory whose window-rattling residents added shrieks, whistles, and a few pairs of underwear to the excitement. Across campus two city fire engines appeared, to extinguish a large wooden cross burning behind the gutted remains of the recently destroyed Kappa Sigma house. Flying rocks and bottles shattered a few car windows, and someone hurled a flaming roll of toilet paper to the roof of Bond Hall. By 1:30 a.m., the rampaging had largely subsided, though shouts and exploding fireworks sporadically punctuated the growing quiet through the rest of the night. Traumatic as the disturbance must have been for school officials, it was puny by national standards and paled even in comparison to an incident the same night 90 miles away where local police sealed off a 20-block area around Jackson State

College as 1500 students seized control of the campus and surrounding area.

But the next night, things turned uglier at Southern. Dean Allen told 1500 students gathered in front of Bennett auditorium that the administration would meet with leaders of the protest the next morning to discuss grievances. By 9:30 all seemed calm. Within an hour, however, the mob again began to grow rowdy. Someone tossed a chain across an electrical transformer, darkening the campus for some time, and eggs began to fly. The crowd seemed to swell and then boil out like spilt liquid into scattered pockets that at times appeared to blanket the entire campus, only to re-form again elsewhere. About 11:30 the students began to converge on the home of the president, who had just returned to town from a speaking engagement. McCain met them near the parking lot behind the Student Services Building and summarily advised them to go home and go to bed. They responded with catcalls and shouts of "duck killer." (One of the more frivolous complaints was that McCain had ordered the slaughter of two ducks, which had actually been returned to Kamper Park from which students had stolen them.) Amid the continued jeers and quacking, someone hurled a light bulb that barely missed the head of the president, who shrugged cooly and finished his talk as several more missiles sailed overhead. After a half hour or so, students began to drift away but reassembled in front of the Hub. Soon after midnight, order returned but not before police had made some twenty arrests for inciting to riot, destruction of property, and resisting arrest.

At ten o'clock the next morning, McCain again met with students, and again they jeered him. Four thousand filed into the coliseum for a ten A.M. convocation to air grievances. Several student spokesmen did precisely that, cataloguing complaints that included bad food, crowded dormitories, mandatory meal tickets, stringent social regulations, and the stifling of free expression. "A primary bone of contention," reported the *Hattiesburg American*, "is that students have had no real voice in the affairs of the university . . . that they are treated as children, told how to dress, where to live, how to act when they have an on-campus date, [and are] forced to room in dormitories they dislike. The list is a long one. Parts of it are silly and parts seem sensible." The president agreed to work with a new faculty-student committee to find mutually acceptable solutions.

Through the early 1960s, campus ROTC as well as American policy in Vietnam remained popular at USM.

The close of the quarter brought calm to the campus, and the new committee, meeting well into the summer, hammered out several proposals, most of which McCain approved. They included relaxation of restrictions on student publications, women's dormitory curfew, off-campus student housing and visitation, and dress codes for men and women. The riots ended in 1967, but there remained a measure of tension between a new generation of students and a president who must have felt betrayed by their apparent indifference to his contributions to the university. Growing national conflicts over racial justice and the Vietnam war heightened these local tensions.

The USM community had generally looked favorably on American efforts in Southeast Asia, as demonstrated by a 1964 campus poll that revealed Barry Goldwater to be the overwhelming student choice in that fall's presidential race. Two years later, support for American policy remained strong. Student leaders early in 1966 secured hundreds of signatures on a petition endorsing the Johnson administration's efforts in Vietnam, and during "G.I. Joe Month" students gave 633 pints of blood to support the war effort.

In 1968 however, the consensus began to erode

Student spokesmen for Hubert Humphrey, Richard Nixon, and George Wallace debate the 1968 presidential election.

at Southern as it did throughout the nation. Press coverage of the enemy's Tet offensive in January etched images of vulnerability, frustration, and defeat upon the consciousness of middle America and fueled the antiwar movement. A student takeover paralyzed Columbia University in the spring, and the summer showdown in Chicago between protesters and Mayor Richard Daley's police at the Democratic National Convention aroused young activists everywhere, including Mississippi. In the fall USM encountered its first real organized dissent in the form of the Student Action Party and its "central committee," the Committee for Student Action. Most students, however, still seemed more interested in the football game against Alabama or Nat's Nook, the new campus coffee house, whose grand opening featured an aspiring young student singer from Mobile, Jimmy Buffett.

But the CSA spawned other dissident groups such as the United Party and the Progressive Student Association, and by early 1969, politics—campus, national, and international; radical, moderate, and reactionary—was fast becoming a favorite student pastime. Dennis White of the Action Party launched a *Student Printz* column "directed at those students who are thoroughly dissatisfied with

American, and especially Southern, society and who are tempted to call themselves 'radicals.'" White dropped out of school after winter quarter but remained active on campus as a distributor of *The Kudzu,* Mississippi's contribution to the era's underground student press. When he defied a school order to remain off campus after business hours, security officers arrested him for trespassing. The administration, White charged, had suppressed "all my attempts to create a more liberal atmosphere and my attempts to win more rights for the students." Dean of men Rader Grantham suggested that White "ought to be in school, or he ought to be out working somewhere. If he's not in school, school matters should not be a concern to him." Student conservatives were also organized and vocal, as reflected by another weekly column, "Slightly to the Right," which a leader of George Wallace's American Independent Youth party contributed to the school newspaper.

Early in 1969 the president of the Interfraternity Council returned from a regional meeting in Miami full of dire warnings about the "menace of the Students for a Democratic Society" with its doctrine of "marxist Communism" and its antipathy toward Greek social organizations. After making

inroads at LSU and Memphis State, the SDS was already moving against Ole Miss, he warned, and with Southern's apathetic student leadership, "this University and this Senate . . . are ripe." Soon afterward, arts and sciences dean Claude Fike echoed the alarm, insisting that the SDS was a "menace and not just a nuisance." Such groups were part of the New Left movement, he warned, and sought "to bring down society in general and the university in particular," thriving on the notion that students possess "a natural right to run the college." A student's only natural right, Fike countered, was "being a student," and he encouraged the campus senators to "raise a student responsibility banner against the student power banner." *The Kudzu* accused USM's campus leaders of ransacking the furniture "in search of leftist gremlins" in a "witch hunt" that constituted "one of the final plays in which ignorance and distrust of the unfamiliar were featured in a heroic role."

By focusing on the student revolt's threat to fraternities and sororities, the controversy ironically drove independent students on the political left and right into each other's arms in a perverse alliance against the Greeks. A fraternity leader observed in the *Student Printz* that "students—es-

Anti-war demonstrations came to Southern in the fall of 1969 as several USM students and faculty participated in the Vietnam Moratorium Day marches, opposite page. Below, members of the campus chapter of the American Civil Liberties Union await a meeting with the president to protest the administration's alleged interference in student government affairs. To some this interstate highway sign, right, symbolized USM in the 1970s. It also gave a new name to the campus grill, far right.

pecially members of the United Party—see SDS as a big, wonderful, revolutionary brother who is about to swoop down and slaughter an imaginary Greek monster." The new student political party, he continued, "would have us believe that Greeks are the sons and daughters of capitalist millionaires—people who drive Cadillacs and hate common people." The response to these charges came not from the political left but from a student spokesman for Wallace's AIY party, who sardonically warned in a newspaper column: "The SDS is coming! The SDS is coming! The SDS is coming!" Invading from LSU in New Orleans, he said, they had been sighted somewhere near Poplarville "headed this way." Fellow travelers lurked everywhere; even the girls in home economics, he noted, were supposedly "cooking up something subversive." While the political passions that spawned the student revolt largely faded with the decade, the SDS scare's prime legacy at USM was a Greek-independent split that remained intense well into the 1970s.

There was also dissension within the faculty. Controversial changes in several departmental chairs and the dismissal of a number of professors provoked cries of repression. A *Hattiesburg Amer-*

ican editorial suggested an investigation of the removal of department heads, and an arts and sciences faculty advisory council accused the administration of "unethical and unprofessional conduct in the intimidation of lawfully and responsibly dissenting faculty members." One disgruntled professor later painted a bleak picture of faculty morale during the late sixties and early seventies. Many of his colleagues, he claimed, had spent those years "under a cloud of dread and with a sense of impending doom. They spoke to each other in whispers. Many were on edge and afraid." Another described Southern as "a twilight zone dominated by the Exit 13 syndrome, a place in which fact and fiction, fantasy and reality all became hopelessly entangled," an institution where "academic freedom or freedom of expression for students and faculty is virtually unheard of." Both of these critics placed their indictments of Southern in a more grandiose context. The former saw "Ft. McCain" as "a microcosmic expression of bureaucratized brutality in American life;" while for the latter, Exit 13 represented "a case study showing how a procapitalist ideology permeates every aspect of college life and curriculum in a way that recreates a microcosm of the authoritarianism,

The deaths of two Jackson State University students in 1970 sparked protests by black students at USM.

racism, and sexism in society itself." And so the political and ideological winds of the age finally drifted over Hattiesburg.

As the end of the sixties approached, the forces of student activism, faculty dissent, and black rights converged. Several professors and black students marched with members of the Progressive Students Association in two antiwar Moratorium Day marches in the fall of 1969. The cooperation extended into the following spring's upheaval over the American military incursion into Cambodia. In the wake of nationwide campus violence that left two Jackson State students—as well as four at Kent State—dead, black activist Julian Bond cancelled an appearance scheduled for May 17 at USM. His telegram message to the sponsoring black students that he assumed the university would "be closed in memory of your slain brothers at Jackson State College" sparked tense demonstrations. The administration issued a statement that "Dr. McCain respects your feelings and is sympathetic with your problems. They are the problems of the entire university and the nation." The president agreed to meet with representatives of the protesters but refused to close the school. Four students were later arrested and suspended from the university

for distributing notices that classes would not meet on May 18 and 19.

The university, which had already instituted a black studies program, intensified its efforts to hire black teachers, and the immediate crisis gradually subsided. Critics continued to complain, however, about the small number of blacks among faculty and administrators, the absence of black fraternities and sororities, and the continued use of what were considered racist symbols: the mascot "General Nat" (Confederate General Nathan Bedford Forrest) and the song "Dixie." General Nat disappeared when Golden Eagles became the school nickname in 1972. The same year, the homecoming court featured a black as senior maid, and in 1974 popular football standout Fred Cook became the first black Mr. USM. Greek social organizations for blacks appeared in 1975: two sororities, Alpha Kappa Alpha and Delta Sigma Theta, and one fraternity, Omega Psi Phi.

Controversy also lingered concerning academic freedom and the role of faculty in university affairs. These seemed to be the pervading concerns of the 1974 report of the Southern Association Committee that visited the campus as part of USM's institutional self-study. The committee

noted a low level of faculty morale, which it blamed on a combination of apathy and insecurity among professors, and recommended the establishment of a faculty senate or some other form of faculty governance. The report also advised either a return to the quarter system or adoption of a semester calendar, as well as the creation of "a tenure system that is clearly defined, guarantees academic freedom, and is in keeping with customary university practice in the nation."

Despite these criticisms, the report had praise for the overall progress of the institution. The visiting committee acknowledged that "the character of the University is changing markedly in the shift from a teacher-training college to a university that is far broader in its mission. The University is deserving of commendation for its efforts to meet the needs of business and industry in the region by developing new programs. Similarly the university has done well in striving to meet local community needs." This assessment underscored USM's enduring effort to adapt its educational mission to the sweeping social changes of modern life without sacrificing the spirit of the institution's original commitment to make life richer for the people of Mississippi.

General Nat, left, gave way to the Golden Eagle as school mascot in 1972. Football star Fred Cook, below left, became the first black Mr. USM in 1974. Walter Washington, below, with President McCain, became the first black to earn a doctoral degree from a Mississippi institution and later became president of Alcorn State University.

Early in 1974 several months before the Southern Association committee visited the campus, McCain announced that he would retire on June 30, 1975. The twenty years of service he gave to the school—more than any president in its history—had been as energetic, forceful, and controversial as the man himself. "Pussycats do not become university presidents," one of his critics later observed," and Dr. McCain was no pussycat. He was . . . a curious, complex man—a walking enigma." A soldier who rose from the enlisted ranks to major general, he could be as cold and hard as steel. In 1972 he boasted before the student senate, "I have worked a long time in this world, and this month I reach complete financial independence, to the extent that I can tell everybody to go to hell." Yet he could be gentle and eloquent, as in his dedication of a genealogical volume: "To the memory of my Father, Samuel Woodward McCain, who taught me the alphabet, and who instilled in me a love for books and for the making of books, and to my Mother, Sarah Alda Shaw McCain, who never said an unkind word to me, who never did an unkind thing toward me, and who never was a party to an unkind act in my presence." He was a humanities scholar who created a separate college

President McCain
through the Years

Enjoying basketball game with students in the 1950s

With grandson in the 1970s

Reviewing ROTC brigade in the 1960s

Changing of the guard—Aubrey Lucas is announced as McCain's successor.

of science and technology at USM and made it one of the university's strongest. He was, as one professor put it, "thoroughly a gentleman," who would never lie. "In my experience with Dr. McCain," said a former dean and long time faculty member, "you could count on his word . . . If you'd go to him and ask for something and he said yes, that yes was firm . . . I do think that's terribly important in an administrator." Yet an *ad hoc* committee of professional historians appointed by the American Historical Association in 1971 concluded that an article that Dr. McCain wrote for a historical

journal "represents a violation of 'approved scholarly usage' with respect to another author's literary property." Some detractors accused him of being too conservative, yet he inaugurated some of the most sweeping changes in the school's history. He steered an institution with a remarkably straitlaced tradition through an era of unparalleled social upheaval with a minimum of disruption. Some of his staunchest supporters thought the tone of his administration was too military. "I was an assistant professor when I came here," said one, "and that would be about the equivalent of corporal. Then I became associate professor, and that was about buck sergeant. Then when I became full professor, I figured that was staff sergeant." Yet even one of his severest critics acknowledged that "the University of Southern Mississippi, on its way to becoming a major academic institution in the South, would not be what it is today had there been no General William D. McCain." He was indeed a complex man, and he served in a complex age.

His final year, as the campus newspaper noted in May 1975, included "some of the most disheartening days of his administrative career." They were haunted by "charges of discrimination—between Greek and Independent, white and black . . . cam-

pus petitions, threats of outside law enforcement agencies on campus . . . [law]suits . . . grand jury investigations . . . [and] a local publicity-hungry district attorney." The disappointments, however, the *Printz* reporter asserted, would never overshadow the achievements. "My goal," McCain said, "was to take a small college and make a good university out of it." The spectacular fulfillment of that goal seems beyond dispute. In 1955 McCain inherited a 3000-student college with an annual appropriation of $2 million. He left a major multipurpose university with more than 11,000 students, 470 full-time faculty—almost 60% of them with terminal degrees—and a $24 million budget. One professor, who first came to Southern in 1926 under Joe Cook, observed that considering "what McCain has done . . . the total picture, how he has developed the organization, its physical facilities . . . increase in staff, great increase in faculty members with terminal degrees, tremendous increase in salaries . . . we must admit or conclude that he is without any reasonable doubt the best we have ever had." R. C. Cook echoed that assessment: "When the annals of the University of Southern Mississippi are written, Dr. W. D. McCain will be listed as the outstanding president of the school."

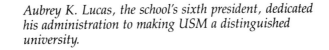

Aubrey K. Lucas, the school's sixth president, dedicated his administration to making USM a distinguished university.

His only fault seemed to be a "superfluous" use of the first person singular. "Years ago he made a talk to the Rotary Club," said Cook, "and the man next to me said after the speech, 'That damn fellow can put more I's into one sentence than any person I have ever known.' Scholar, soldier, and administrator that he is, maybe he is entitled to spread a few personal pronouns around."

When the board of trustees in October 1974, named Aubrey K. Lucas to succeed him, McCain seemed pleased. "We need him now. We've gone through two decades of bitter, bitter battles; I fit into the battles, he'll fit into the peaceful world." Asked what influence he hoped to have on the new administration, McCain said he intended to keep any advice to himself. After all, he explained, "No one told me anything when I came here."

*A*ubrey Keith Lucas was no stranger to Hattiesburg. A native of State Line, he received a bachelor's and a master's degree from Mississippi Southern College before earning a Ph.D. from Florida State University in 1966. He served USM as director of admissions, registrar, and dean of the graduate school, as well as professor of education,

before leaving in 1971 for Delta State University where he became a respected and immensely popular president. In July 1975, Lucas returned to his alma mater as its sixth president.

Two months later he delivered an important address that contained a blueprint for what would unfold during the first dozen years of his leadership. It began with a word of gratitude, cloaked in a sample of the disarming sense of humor that would stand him in good stead during the more tense moments of those twelve years. Speaking to a faculty eager for some insight into the tone of the incoming administration, he gave thanks for the hospitality they had shown since his arrival. "Your friendliness and helpfulness . . . have been matched only by your advice and counsel," he added, "all of which I need, and some of which I even appreciate." Aware that the role of the faculty in university affairs was a serious matter, however, Lucas noted that "goal setting *is* important, for truly if we have no vision, we shall perish with aimless wanderings or debilitating arguing and struggling over priorities." Yet he intended only to "sketch broadly here, not because I think specifics are unimportant, but because I believe all of you ought to have some part in planning this institu-

tion's future by filling in details through appropriate committee and council work." Those must have been welcome words to his listeners, who heard him go on to speak of "consensus decision making," meaning not that "we consult with everybody or that we vote on every issue," but that he expected his administrators to "be prepared to defend our decisions, and . . . be big enough to modify them if they turn out to be bad ones."

In that initial address, Lucas articulated what would become the theme of his administration. "We must set for ourselves," he said, "no less goal than to become a *distinguished* university. I believe that we can be, and I believe that we ought to serve notice on our competitors and our constituencies that we intend to be so." Distinction had to begin, he insisted, with the faculty, which is "the very heart and soul of a university." That meant first of all careful selection. "It is my intention," he revealed, "to interview every prospect. I have asked the deans to search carefully into the backgrounds of faculty to make sure that they are productive scholars who are willing to work hard to help us achieve our goals." But securing good teachers would not be enough; "we need to nurture our faculty," he continued, and "find ways and means

to reward them properly. It is my goal that the faculty of this university shall be the highest paid in our state."

The new president went on to outline other goals: "establishing an honors college" to attract "the brightest students in our state and region;" creating "opportunities for our students to study abroad;" strengthening the library, going "beyond books [to] develop a learning center where all kinds of instructional aids are available;" and reassessing "our present credit-calendar system." One of the obvious tasks Lucas faced was reconciling the new vision of distinction with the school's career orientation. "I am well aware," he noted, "that there are those in the faculty who feel that the career university and the distinguished university are incompatible . . . It seems to me that we can define and structure career opportunities in such a way that our larger goal of eminence will be enhanced." Much of the first decade of the Lucas era would be spent refining that definition and structure.

"In 1952," Lucas concluded, "I came here from State Line as green a freshman as was ever admitted, expecting and needing a lot and I was not disappointed. In 1975, I'm back, somewhat awed

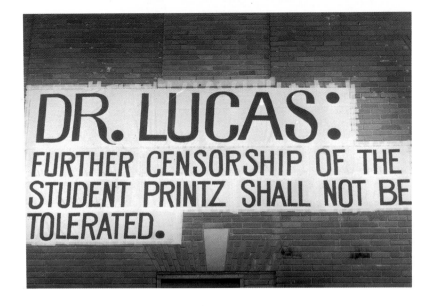

Student dissent faded in the late seventies but did not disappear.

by the challenge but confident that with the great talent assembled here dedicated to conspicuous excellence and to bringing about a true academic community, we will become a distinguished university."

It was student life, however, rather than faculty or curriculum, to which the new administration turned its attention first. Students returned in that fall of 1975 to discover a streamlined rules system that granted self-regulating hours to all female dormitory residents and the right to live off-campus to all students over twenty-one years of age. Though the regulations explicitly forbade possession, consumption, or sale of alcoholic beverages on campus, they eliminated university restrictions regarding the use of alcohol by students off-campus, yielding that responsibility strictly to the administration of local law. So almost a decade after USM students "rioted" to protest being told "where to live and how to act," the university finally placed its "boys and girls" in fact where Joe Cook, more than sixty years earlier, had put them in principle: "on their own responsibility."

A year later Lucas reorganized the school's student affairs division, with financial aid, housing, placement, special services, and counseling affairs under a dean of student services, Charles Probst, and the counseling center, office of religious affairs, university union, and student activities under a dean of student development, Max McDaniel. Discipline functions and campus security remained under dean of men Rader Grantham, who, with the two new deans, reported to vice president for student affairs Peter Durkee.

In the summer of 1976 the president appointed an *ad hoc* committee to investigate charges of a "double standard" in the university's application of judicial procedures. Some independent students complained that Greek students and organizations were subject to Panhellenic and Interfraternity Council judicial boards rather than the university's student affairs committee. Early in 1977 Lucas approved a restructuring of judicial procedures that explicitly protected students' "right to privacy" in their living quarters and established a single discipline system for all students and campus organizations. Despite the controversy, the president insisted that he found no widespread student dissatisfaction, and indeed the new generation of students did seem to be more sedate and content than those of the previous decade. The arrival of

two new black fraternities, Kappa Alpha Psi and Alpha Phi Alpha, in 1976 attested to both the continued vitality and growing diversity of campus Greek life.

Athletics also remained popular. Bobby Collins's first football squad, again playing all its games on the road, finished 7-4, winning more games than any Southern team in a decade. His second team finished 2-9, losing more games than any in school history. A 48-point shutout by East Carolina on opening day began a nine-game losing skid that included a 63-19 pounding by Brigham Young and an embarrassing 28-0 loss to Ole Miss before a capacity crowd in the inaugural game in new M. M. Roberts stadium. The misery finally ended with a 14-12 upset over Memphis State. That game in some sense marked the real beginning of Eagle Fever as a small but vocal home crowd vented a season's worth of frustration in a loud and raucous display of home town support that echoed into the next week, a win over Texas-Arlington, and the next year. There was more to the silver lining than merely a pair of belated victories. Through the dark cloud of 1976 at times glimmered several characteristics that both echoed past glory and forecast future success. One was a punishing

M. M. Roberts, flanked here by President Lucas and Governor Cliff Finch, dedicates USM's new football stadium named in his honor in 1976. Roberts received a diploma from Mississippi Normal College in 1917 and returned to earn a Ph.D. from USM in 1964. As president of the state college board during the 1960s, he did much to advance Southern's interests.

ground attack that became a hallmark of Bobby Collins football, typified by tailback Ben Garry who would amass during his career at Southern more rushing yardage (3595) than any collegiate player in Mississippi history, including Walter Payton. The second trait was a ferocious defense anchored by a group of linebackers who brought back memories of P. W. Underwood's Vandals of the early sixties. They became known as the Nasty Bunch, and in 1978, when Collins hired his former North Carolina colleague Jim Carmody as defensive coordinator, the defense adopted him as the original Big Nasty. A final characteristic of the 1976 Eagles was a reinvigorated USM tradition of doggedly determined play by athletes with marginal

athletic ability but with a wealth of character and grit. The victory over Memphis State was engineered by a sophomore quarterback from Memphis who ironically drew his first starting assignment against the home-town school that had passed him over in recruiting. Jeff Hammond's unspectacular but steady play that night not only helped break Southern's frustrating losing streak, it also cost the Tigers a bowl invitation. Hammond was one of a seemingly endless stream of Golden Eagles stalwarts who came to USM because no one else seemed to think they could play college football.

The climb to respectability began in 1977 when Collins's crew defeated Auburn, Ole Miss, and Mississippi State (the first of seven in a row against the Bulldogs) to enter a solid claim to the college championship of Mississippi and a somewhat less serious one to the SEC title. A late season slump that included consecutive losses to Louisiana Tech and Arkansas State turned what began as a remarkable season into a mediocre 6-6.

The next year when Collins' first recruiting class became seniors, his program finally turned the corner. Ironically, the pivotal game was a loss, one of three non-victories that Collins would later de-

scribe as among the most important in his tenure at USM. Before a huge crowd in Jackson, Southern and Ole Miss found themselves locked in a 13-13 stalemate when the Eagles began a drive with barely three minutes left in the game. On third down and one at the Ole Miss 36 yard line, junior quarterback Dane McDaniel sprinted left to find an open field to the first down in front of him. Needing only a field goal to win, he started to run when he spotted Chuck Carr Brown running free behind the defensive secondary and lofted a pass that fell just short enough for 6'4" Rebel cornerback John Fabris to leap and clutch with a heartbreaking interception that he would have returned for a touchdown had Eagle reserve James Hale not bolted from the USM sidelines in bitter frustration to take him down short of the goal line. Despite the penalty for Hale's desperate tackle from the bench, Ole Miss had to settle for a field goal, but it was enough for a crushing 16-13 win. The following week, however, McDaniel redeemed himself, leading his teammates to a 22-17 victory over Mississippi State on their way to a 7-4 finish.

The Golden Eagles closed the seventies with a 6-4-1 season that included memorable games against Florida State, Ole Miss, Tulane, and Arkan-

The resurgence of USM football in the late 1970s spawned enthusiasm in various forms: scarce game tickets, which students secured by camping out at ticket booths, below, and others secured by any means available, left; and increased community support exemplified by unofficial cheerleaders like Ray Crawford, below left, known to Eagle fans as "Two-Bits."

Ben Garry, shown here against Auburn in 1977, rushed for more yards than any player in Mississippi collegiate football history.

sas State. In the season opener in Tallahassee, the Eagles came within a whisker of upsetting a highly ranked Seminole team that would win all of its regular season games on the way to the Orange Bowl. A blocked punt and a punt return for a touchdown, both in the final quarter, allowed FSU to escape with a 17-14 win. The Ole Miss game was memorable because of a newly-installed I-formation that ground the Rebels into submission 38-8 to avenge the previous year's disappointing loss. The Tulane game was another of those non-victories that proved so important in USM's quest for football distinction. Aided by two crucial pass interference penalties, quarterback Roch Hontas marched the Green Wave 67 yards to take a 20-19 lead with 44 seconds left in the game. A furious Eagle comeback effort—which included a 90-yard cross-field lateral and run nullified by a penalty—fell short with Winston Walker's 41 yard field goal attempt that left the home crowd sitting in stunned silence. Despite the outcome, the game was perhaps the most thrilling ever played on campus and did much to generate a loyal and enthusiastic constituency for Roberts Stadium football. The game against Arkansas State was notable not so much for

the 14-6 victory that ended the season as for the debut of quarterback Reggie Collier, whose lithe limbs at times took on the appearance of a young colt. But over the next three years Collins molded the youngster from D'Iberville into a supple and steady thoroughbred who carried Eagle football fortunes to their pinnacle. Collier not only broke a host of school offensive records, he solidified what Willie Heidelburg had begun a decade before, manfully demonstrating, not only that a black athlete could exercise capable leadership, but that white athletes would follow it and white fans would applaud it. No football program in the South has done more for racial harmony than Southern's, and for that Bobby Collins and Reggie Collier deserve much credit.

A new era of Golden Eagle basketball also began under Aubrey Lucas when Memphis State assistant M. K. Turk replaced Jeep Clark as head coach in 1976. It took Turk but two seasons to carve USM's first winning record (13-12) since 1969–70. After a 13-14 season the next year, his troops posted a 17-10 mark in 1979–80, barely missing the school's first National Invitational Tournament bid by dropping its last two games, both by one point.

True Grit

*P*erhaps no USM player embodied the character of Eagle football as did Sammy Winder. He was the supreme over-achiever. The last of eleven children born to sharecroppers Henry and Norcuss Winder, he faced enormous obstacles in securing a college education. He spent much of his youth hauling hay and chasing cows on the family's rented farm near Pocahontas in southwest Madison County and walked a mile each day to catch the local school bus, which could reach his house only with great difficulty. But football changed things for Winder,

though there were still days when, as his high school coach recalled, "Sammy came up to me and said, "Coach, I don't know if I can be at practice today, because I've got to pull corn." Valuable as he was to the Madison-Ridgeland High School team—valuable enough that the school bus finally found a way to get to his house, at least on dry days—college scouts seemed uninterested. But Sammy was determined not only to play college football but to get a degree. "I want an education," he later told a reporter during his USM days. "I remember the guys

I hung out with in Pocahontas. Some of them were faster and better than me, but they didn't want to go to college, [though] they had the opportunity. I didn't want to do that. They'd have to run me out to get me out of here." With that kind of determination, Winder walked on at USM, eventually earned a scholarship, and became one of the most productive ball carriers in school history. He went on to a successful career in professional football during which he helped lead the Denver Broncos to the 1987 Super Bowl and appeared on the cover of *Sports Illustrated*. But the picture of Sammy Winder that Eagle fans will always remember was the magnificent leaping touchdown against Ole Miss in 1980, left, because it so perfectly captures the character of the man and the team that carried Eagle football fortunes to their grandest heights.

Kay James, far left, became Lady Eagle basketball coach in 1976, and by 1980 USM varsity athletics included women's volleyball and softball as well as basketball.

Despite the disappointment, M. K. Turk's Eagles entered the 1980s poised on the brink of basketball prominence.

A year after Turk came, Lucas and Roland Dale brought another basketball coach to Southern. Gulfport native Kay James became the school's first fulltime women's basketball coach, taking over a program that USM had revived in 1975 after an absence of almost 50 years. That first squad finished with a disappointing 5-14 record, but the Lady Eagles then reeled off nine straight winning seasons, eight of them under Coach James. By 1980 Dale had also added men's swimming, indoor and outdoor track, and cross country, as well as women's volleyball and softball to an athletic program that began to reflect USM's emergence as a major state university.

That status was also reflected in enrollment, which by the end of the seventies was over 12,000, more than 10,000 on the main campus alone. The summer "Mini-Quarter" became a popular and successful fixture of student orientation. These pre-registration sessions helped new students adjust to the full range of life at Southern through meetings with deans, department chairmen, student leaders, and representatives of campus organ-

izations. Of the 8713 freshmen and transfers who participated in the program between 1976 and 1980, more than 95% returned as regular students in the fall.

*D*uring his first year in office, Lucas also reorganized the university's administrative structure by instituting a system of vice-presidents. Dean Charles Moorman became vice-president for academic affairs; Peter Durkee, vice-president of student affairs; Thomas G. Estes, vice-president for business and finance; and Shelby Thames, vice-president for administration and regional campuses. Gary C. Wildmon replaced Thames as dean of science and technology, and Onva K. Boshears became dean of a new school of library science that was established in 1976, the first such program to

be accredited in Mississippi. James Sims replaced Claude Fike, who resigned as dean of liberal arts in 1976. Lucas appointed two other deans during the 1977–78 year: Shirley Jean Jones of the graduate school of social work and John L. Green of fine arts, which had become a college in 1975. In 1978 Bobby D. Anderson replaced Eric Gunn as dean of education and psychology. Other personnel changes included Wallace Kay as dean of the Honors College (1978), Clyde Ginn as dean of extension and public service (1976), and Eugene Saucier as dean of administration and special academic services (1976).

In the second year of his administration, Lucas approved a new 32-member, elected Faculty Council "to provide for the faculty," according to its charter, "both a forum and a voice and so allow it to assert for the general welfare of the University its distinctive viewpoint and principles." In September 1978, the university ended a fifty-two-year tradition when it abandoned the quarter calendar and adopted a full semester system. Lucas approved the change, he said, "after long deliberation and . . . countless reports and discussions involving all areas of the university." As expected, the faculty generally applauded the new format,

Burgeoning enrollment sometimes produced a shortage of campus housing that the university dealt with in novel ways as illustrated by this Housing Office display at registration. The remodeled President's Home, below, became the Alumni House in 1976. Noted English scholar Geoffrey Ashe, opposite page, lectures to students of USM's British Studies Program at castle ruins associated with Arthurian legend.

but it proved very unpopular among students at first. Nonetheless, as Lucas reported to the board in 1979, USM "made the transition . . . with very little trouble." In fact, the requisite reworking of class lectures, reexamination of procedures, and adjustments in class schedules produced "an updated curriculum, a trimmed-down schedule, and a computerized registration system," all of which proved quite beneficial.

Curriculum changes included new or expanded emphasis programs in paralegal studies, safety education, and environmental design; a new school of professional accountancy, designation of music as a school; graduate programs in nursing, library science, and counseling and clinical psychology. Accreditation of programs by recognized national professional agencies became a major goal in the pursuit of academic excellence, and programs that earned initial accreditation after 1975 included dietetics, professional accountancy, art, art education, dance, theatre, interior design, corrective therapy, journalism, athletic administration and coaching, social work, physical education, psychology, counseling psychology, business, home economics education, and librarianship. Engineering technology blossomed into one of the univer-

The new R. C. Cook University Union, which opened in 1976, included a spot for Cecil's newspaper stand, right, which had long been a fixture at the campus grill.

sity's showpieces with accredited programs in architectural, construction, computer, electronics, industrial, and mechanical engineering technology.

Another significant innovation was the university's program in international education, which began in the summer of 1976 when the department of criminal justice sent 26 students to England for a first-hand study of British criminal law and procedures. The program soon expanded to include economics, philosophy, political science, sociology, history, finance, English, and library science and by 1979 was exposing more than 60 students from 29 states to the instruction of an array of prominent British scholars in those fields. Meanwhile, the Honors College Forum series brought distinguished speakers to the Hattiesburg campus, including John Barth, Howard Nemerov, George Gilder, Garry Wills, Phyllis Schlafly, Benjamin Hooks, Jerry Rubin, Charles Kuralt, and former British Prime Minister Sir Harold Wilson. The university also sponsored two major symposia that featured nationally recognized lecturers: "Images '79: A Focus on Women;" and "Mississippi: A Sense of Place."

The dust of McCain's construction boom still

swirled even after he moved out of the Dome, as Lucas supervised the completion of several major projects that had begun under his predecessor. These included a new physical plant facility, a speech and hearing building, the McCain Graduate Library, the new Cook University Union, and a $6 million expansion of the football stadium (named for M. M. Roberts) to a capacity of 33,000, all of which opened in 1976. Other construction included a new president's home (1979), the C. W. Woods Art Gallery (1979), the Bobby L. Chain Technology Building (1980), and major renovations of the old president's home (which became the Alumni House in 1976), McLemore Hall, several physical plant facilities, the printing center, the football field house (funded by a private donation), as well as Hattiesburg, Mississippi, and Hickman dormitories. Also a new Teaching-Learning Resource Center opened in 1976 with equipment for a three-color-camera studio, a graphics service, a non-print media preview service, and a program of faculty renewal and improvement seminars.

The invigorated quest for academic excellence placed a special emphasis on faculty research and publication. During the 1978–79 year, fifteen members of the college of science and technology were

invited to present scholarly papers at professional meetings abroad, as were representatives of fine arts, liberal arts, and business administration. Faculty scholarship increased steadily after 1975 and in the first year of the school's seventh decade reached an unprecedented 54 books, 516 articles in scholarly journals, more than 300 papers delivered at professional meetings, and 20 exhibitions of creative art. For the year, the faculty also generated more than $3.5 million dollars in research grants from agencies outside the university.

None of this diminished the institution's fundamental commitment, which remained quality education for the people of Mississippi. As vice-president for academic affairs Charles Moorman later put it, "We thought that if a man or a woman gave himself wholeheartedly to his profession in terms of teaching, then he would become automatically

Vice President for Academic Affairs Charles W. Moorman

involved in research. But first and always was teaching—first and always was the idea of training the students, teaching the students to go out into the world and become profitable and useful members of society, and sensitive citizens." And so the dream remained what it had been for almost seven decades, but those early dreamers would have been astounded to see the great university that their beloved little normal college had become. Like those oak seedlings that Joe Cook nurtured so carefully so many years before, the University of Southern Mississippi had, despite the scars of struggle and pruning, blossomed into luxuriant maturity. "No one could have dreamed," said President Emeritus McCain, "that we could have gone from a small teachers college to a major university in less than seventy-five years. No one could have dreamed that."

The Sehoy Story

For years the large tract of Lamar County land that J. J. Newman Lumber Company donated to MNC in 1910 lay largely undeveloped. Officially designated the college farm, it came to the attention of English Professor Wilbur W. Stout in the mid-1950s. As a graduate student at the University of North Carolina, Stout had become acquainted with Frederick Koch's Carolina Playmakers, especially their productions of outdoor folk theatre. After coming to Southern Stout hoped to develop a similar outdoor drama patterned after Paul Green's "The Lost Colony" or Kermit Hunter's popular Cherokee epic "Unto These Hills." Amidst the tall pines of the long neglected farm, he found an ideal natural amphitheatre and persuaded President McCain to help him develop it. Beginning in 1956 the college slowly transformed the site into an attractive recreation area that included a 40-acre lake. The outdoor theatre never materialized, though retired army colonel and MSC graduate student E. A. Wink wrote a script, "Red Eagle," an Indian saga based on the early settlement of the Mississippi territory. In the late fifties, when construction of Pinehaven apartments destroyed the old golf course, a new one was built just south of Lake Sehoy, as the new lake was called in honor of the Creek Indian princess who was a leading character in Wink's play. In 1979 an outdoor recreational complex was constructed adjacent to the lake which is still known as Lake Sehoy.

Toward Distinction

The Eighties and Beyond

In 1981 Mississippi's Board of Trustees of Institutions of Higher Learning issued mission statements to the eight public universities under its jurisdiction. The unbridled boom in education had peaked in the early 1970s, and gone were the days when the state seemed awash with money and university expansion appeared unlimited. In a period of growing austerity, the board was attempting to improve higher education by establishing a "direction of excellence" for each university within "differential roles" clearly defined among them. Designating USM, along with Ole Miss and Mississippi State, as a "comprehensive" institution, the board assigned to it leadership roles in communications, computer science, home economics, library science, marine sciences, music, polymer science, psychology, social work, and technology. These designations indicated that the board expected Southern to pursue regional and national distinction in its leadership fields while maintaining the quality of its other established programs and continuing to be a center for the "development of new knowledge and the expansion of existing research."

Approaching its seventy-fifth anniversary, then, USM defined itself as "an emerging, comprehen-

sive institution committed to seek and reward distinction among its programs, faculty, students, and services. Its purposes are to provide high-quality teaching, research, and service for the benefit of the people of Mississippi, the Gulf South, and the nation." Into the 1980s the university continued to prosper as it pursued those goals.

In 1982 another administrative reorganization took place. Vice-presidents for business and finance and student affairs remained basically as they were. A vice-president for research and extended services (Karen Yarbrough) replaced the vice-president for administration and regional campuses and, with the vice-president for academic affairs, now reported to the president through a new executive vice-president, Shelby Thames. The extra layer of bureaucracy provoked some complaints of blurred lines of responsibility, delays in decision-making, and centralized authority and led to some efforts to streamline the system, but as a Southern Association committee reported in 1985, the new scheme seemed "to be appropriate for the changing character of the institution." In 1983 James Sims replaced Charles Moorman as vice-president for academic affairs, and Terry Harper became dean of liberal arts. Sev-

eral other new deans took office in the early eighties: Jerri Laube in nursing, David Huffman in science and technology, James Schnur in education and psychology, Tyrone Black in business administration, Peggy Prenshaw in honors, and Allene Vaden in home economics. In other changes Clyde Ginn became executive assistant to the president, Eugene Tinnon dean of extension and public service, and Joseph Paul dean of student development. In 1986 Shelby Thames resigned as vice-president and returned to fulltime teaching in polymer science.

Responding to the college board's new policy, Lucas in 1982 designated communications, computer science, and marine science as areas in which the university would develop "centers of excellence." The board policy was then to provide specific financial resources to allow these programs to pursue particular regional and national recognition. Those efforts suffered a minor setback when the trustees, amid great controversy, removed USM's leadership roles in journalism and computer science in 1984.

The board defended its action as a response to academic program reviews that it had commissioned the universities to conduct in connection

The USM English department's Center for Writers under Director Frederick Barthelme, right, became one of only a handful in the nation to offer master's and Ph.D. degrees in creative writing. Movie rights to two of Barthelme's own critically acclaimed novels were purchased by major production companies, Second Marriage *by Twentieth Century Fox and* Tracer *by Steppenwolf Theatre Company.*

with the 1981 mission statements. Lucas, who had been out of town when the board made its decision, found himself squeezed between the USM community, especially an outraged faculty, and the trustees to whom he was constitutionally accountable. It was probably the most difficult issue of his presidency, and despite obviously severe personal disappointment, he refused to question the trustees' motives. "It's been a tough one," he acknowledged, "because I like my board. They're good people." Though his public response to the decision, according to a Jackson newspaper, "wasn't warmly received" by the board, many among the faculty were disappointed that he did not confront the trustees even more aggressively. Lucas suggested using the program reviews to reexamine the assignment of other leadership roles, in which case, he argued, "surely the board will assign to USM leadership in English, history, philosophy, anthropology, geography, medical technology, mathematics, speech and hearing science, and perhaps even biology," all of which had initially gone to other institutions. The reviews "imply and in some cases state," he said, that USM offered Mississippi's best programs in those areas.

The outside consultants had indeed given high marks to several Southern programs that did not

receive leadership designations:

Graduates of the program are well trained and highly sought after by local and regional industry (chemistry).

It is evident that USM has an exceptional program that ranks highly in national competition (medical technology).

This is an excellent program with good balance (mathematics).

This is the best undergraduate program in the state (philosophy).

This is perhaps the best undergraduate program in the state (history).

Moreover, USM was the only institution whose programs received no "approval pending," "marginal," or "phase-out" ratings in the review process. Every one of its seventy-four undergraduate programs received an "approval" rating, and three—English, polymer science, and medical technology—earned "commendations," indicating the board's recognition that in those fields USM ranked among the nation's best.

Though the board made no other leadership changes, USM overcame the losses, and its centers of excellence prospered. In 1985 all four emphases in journalism—news-editorial, advertising, photo-

journalism, and public relations—received full accreditation, making USM one of only fourteen programs in the nation to share that distinction. The same year, the school lured a nationally recognized marine biologist to direct the center for marine science, which at the same time moved its facilities to the National Space Technologies Laboratory near Bay St. Louis, strengthening its relationship to the prominent marine science community there.

In 1981 USM created a Center for International Education which assumed direction of the English Language Institute, the Office of International Student Admissions and Advisement, the Institute for Anglo-American Studies, and the Office of International Studies. The ELI served more than seven thousand students from forty nations in the decade after 1975, and foreign student enrollment at the university jumped by more than two hundred percent between 1981 and 1984. By the mid-1980s the OIS was taking more than 300 students each summer to study geology in Switzerland's Jura Mountains, Germany's Black Forest, and the Tel Kinneret in Israel; the clothing industry in Paris, Milan, and Zurich; anthropology in Mexico's Yucatan; as well as bringing noted European scholars to teach students on the Hattiesburg campus. The British Studies Program in 1983 offered more

than twenty-six courses that encompassed lectures by English senior artists, scholars, business leaders, and civil servants; research in prominent British museums and repositories; and special seminars and tutorials under the supervision of USM faculty.

Southern broadened its services to non-traditional students, as the division of continuing education became the division of lifelong learning in 1985. Its adult studies program, through expanded evening class offerings and a competent counseling staff afforded working adults the opportunity to pursue a degree part-time, prepare for an alternate career, or simply develop themselves culturally and intellectually. The independent study program offered a complete high school curriculum as well as almost one hundred university-level courses. The department of on-campus non-credit sponsored a variety of camps and clinics, conferences, workshops, institutes, seminars, and other services to employees of business and industry and other professional people, as well as a full array of non-credit courses for the general public. Though the university was forced to close its Natchez branch in 1985, USM-Gulf Park continued to thrive with a steady enrollment of well over 1000.

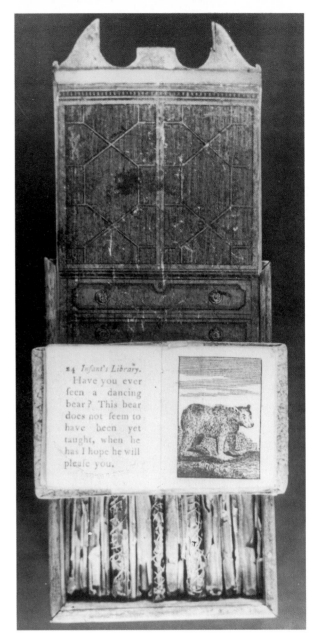

By the mid-1980s, USM libraries contained almost a million volumes. Among the McCain Library and Archives' special collections is the world renowned de Grummond Children's Literature Research Collection, which includes The Infants Library, *above, a collection of 16 miniature books published in London in 1800.*

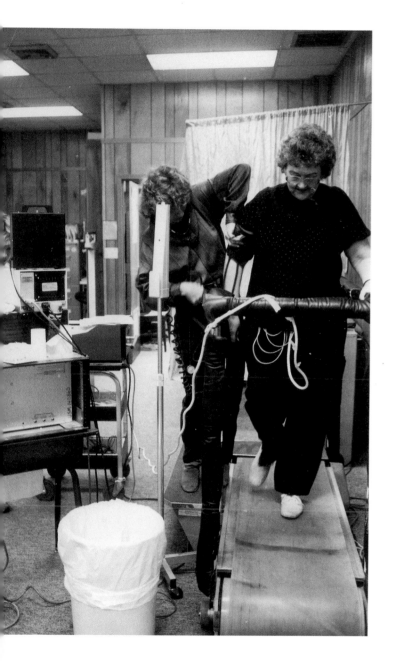

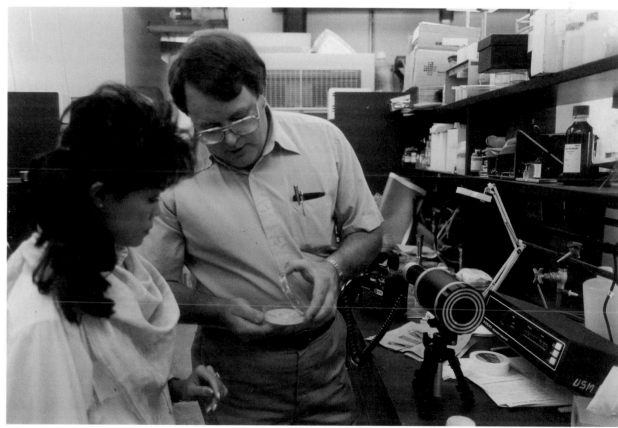

During 1984–85 USM installed a new mainframe computer and hired a staff consultant to facilitate faculty and staff access to its benefits. At the same time the administration initiated a computer augmented curriculum to increase the use of computer technology in all disciplines of study. A computerized system of pre-registration began in 1986, simplifying registration for students and administration alike.

Since its origin in 1959, the USM Foundation had by 1985 raised more than $15 million to support scholarships and other academic needs. Nineteen eighty-one was the first million dollar year, and by 1986 annual income had reached $3 million. In 1985 a seventy-fifth anniversary campaign was launched to raise $7.5 million by the end of 1987. In an era of growing fiscal austerity, the university recognized that "private financial support is the critical margin between a good university and a great one." In 1987 USM named Don Elam fulltime director of development and commissioned him to further the university's programs and services through planned resource development, focusing on business, foundations, industry, and individuals.

The Golden Eagles captured the mythical state football championship by defeating both Ole Miss and Mississippi State in 1977, 1979, 1980, and 1983.

*D*uring the eighties, USM's athletic program also rose to new heights. The 1980 football team celebrated the dawning of the decade with the school's network television debut, the first bowl invitation since 1957, and the third mythical state championship in four years. The season opened with a 17-14 win over Tulane in the New Orleans Superdome that ABC televised regionally. Later, after a 28-22 victory over Ole Miss in Jackson, Collins marched his troops to Starkville in quest of a second consecutive sweep of the two Mississippi rivals. "The game should have been rated R," wrote Jackson columnist Orley Hood, "children under 17 not admitted without parent or guardian. Southern Mississippi 42, Mississippi State 14 . . . It was about as one-sided as the St. Valentine's Day Massacre . . . There was nothing graceful about it . . . Nothing subtle . . . The Golden Eagles drove up the road, beat the hell out of the Bulldogs, and went home. It was hit-and-run, but it was no accident. Nothing personal, you know, just business." Sammy Winder rushed for three touchdowns on his way to the national scoring title, and Southern ran its record to 5-0 for the season and 7-1 against in-state competition since 1976. "How good is Southern?" asked Hood. "The best in Mississippi . . . It's not even close."

In 1981 Reggie Collier became the first college quarterback ever to rush and pass for 1000 yards in a single season and finished ninth in the voting for the Heisman Trophy.

It was a different matter when the Eagles ventured outside the Magnolia State. After drubbing Arkansas State 35-0 in Hattiesburg the next week, holding the Indians to nineteen total yards and a single first down, Southern crept into the number twenty slot in the Associated Press poll and headed for Birmingham to challenge the top-ranked Crimson Tide. Alabama ended Southern's visit to the top twenty after only a week, crushing Collins' crew 42-7. Two weeks later Auburn added to the chastening with a 31-0 rout, and the Eagles stumbled to an 8-3 finish, losing the final game against Louisville 6-3 in a freezing drizzle. But that was good enough for a trip to Shreveport's Independence Bowl, which the Eagles won 16-14 over McNeese State to give the school its first post-season victory in five tries.

The next season proved even better. After four straight wins early in the year, Collins again took his team to Birmingham undefeated. Exactly twenty-five years after the same two teams had battled to a 13–13 tie in Tuscaloosa, Steve Clark kicked a field goal with eight seconds left to make 1981's score identical to that of 1956 and once again draw the nation's attention to Southern football. A month later a capacity crowd filed into Jackson's Memorial Stadium to watch one of the most impor-

The 1981 USM-Mississippi State football game in Jackson's Memorial Stadium set a record for the largest attendance at an event in Mississippi sports history.

The legendary Bear Bryant congratulates Coach Jim Carmody after the Eagles ended Alabama's 19-year home winning streak in 1982.

tant games in Mississippi college football history, as USM and Mississippi State met with bowl invitations and national rankings on the line. It was a bruising defensive battle reminiscent of the 10-9 State victory in 1966. A Winder touchdown offset two Dana Moore field goals to give the Eagles a 7-6 lead at the half. The Nasty Bunch made that one point hold up, stopping the Bulldogs twice in the fourth quarter on fourth down and less than a yard.

The slim victory nudged Southern back into the top twenty as they headed for Tallahassee to play Florida State in a regional telecast, which ABC interrupted periodically to cover the return of NASA's space shuttle. And as *Columbia* touched down in California, the Eagles were taking flight in Florida, in equally spectacular fashion, scoring on their first seven possessions to humiliate a Seminole team that had earlier beaten Ohio State in Columbus and Notre Dame at South Bend. The 58-14 score was shocking, and it catapulted USM into the top ten (ninth in AP, eighth in UPI) for the first time in history. Louisville brought the Eagles back to earth with a 13-10 upset the following week, and a 19-17 Tangerine Bowl loss to Missouri knocked them out of the national rankings com-

pletely. But 1981 had been a remarkable year, especially for Collier who finished ninth in balloting for the Heisman Trophy and became the first college quarterback ever both to rush and pass for 1000 yards in the same season.

Less than a month after the Tangerine Bowl, Bobby Collins accepted the head coaching position at Southern Methodist University where six of nine USM assistants joined him. In a matter of hours, Dale replaced Collins with Big Nasty himself, former assistant head ·coach and defensive coordinator Jim Carmody. The new Eagle boss had played at Tulane where he earned both bachelor's and master's degrees. He first came to USM in 1978 after serving as an assistant at Tulane, Kentucky, Mississippi State, North Carolina, and Ole Miss. After three years at Southern, he became defensive line coach for the NFL's Buffalo Bills for a year before returning to take over from Collins.

Carmody inherited a solid football program, but he also inherited allegations of a recruiting scandal that for two years had hung over that program like a pall. "The first day I reported for work," he later recalled, "the NCAA was here." The distractions aggravated the normal difficulties involved in a major coaching change and took a heavy toll early

in Carmody's first season. But after a 1-3 start, the Eagles reeled off five consecutive wins and appeared to be on their way to a third straight bowl invitation. Then the NCAA ax fell, and it was crushing. On the Monday before the Alabama game, USM announced that recruiting violations, some involving "promises of significant financial benefits to prospective athletes," between 1979 and 1982 had resulted in a two-year probation that included sanctions against television and bowl appearances. "This is an embarrassment to me as president," Lucas told reporters. "I wish we didn't have to drink from this cup." Dale shouldered the blame himself, but as Lucas pointed out, none of the infractions even remotely involved the athletic director. "We must remember," the president cautioned, "that the NCAA did not take note of his standards. He is a man of integrity." Nonetheless, Dale acknowledged that "somebody has to be responsible, and I am."

It was a bitter pill for Carmody and his players, who found themselves at a crossroads. "We're going to go out and practice hard and keep our heads up," the coach insisted. "I hope the football team will rise to the challenge." And indeed they did. In a remarkable display of coaching skill, Car-

mody and his staff turned adversity to their advantage, transforming the Alabama contest into the Eagles' own private bowl. USM handed Bear Bryant his first defeat in Tuscaloosa in fifty-seven games—and incidentally wreaked some sweet but belated revenge for the 64-point embarrassment that Pie Vann had suffered at the hands of a much younger Bryant thirty-three years before. Reggie Collier had perhaps his finest hour, engineering three first-quarter touchdowns, two on brilliant runs of his own that left Tide defenders clutching space that he had long since vacated on his way to the Alabama end zone. Selma native Sam Dejarnette, who was barely a year old when Florida upended Bryant's 1963 squad 10-6 for his only other loss in Denny Stadium, finally turned in an outstanding performance on his home soil, rushing for 152 yards and two touchdowns. And the Nasty Bunch turned back a furious Tide rally in the second half to preserve the 39-28 victory. It was a vintage USM upset that epitomized the best in a long tradition of Southern football. "This win proved to everyone," Carmody beamed, "the kind of youngsters we have at Southern Mississippi." Mickey Spagnola described them well in his *Jackson Daily News* postmortem of the Alabama home win

streak. "If you're going to war," he wrote, "and if you get to pick first, choose Southern Mississippi. Always choose Southern Mississippi . . . Don't fight Southern Mississippi. No matter how hard you fight, those folks will fight harder. They are that way, as if this Hattiesburg, this school of 11,800, is some sort of transplanted inner-city core in the state of Mississippi. Blue collar types, you know. Hard hats, tatoos . . . These people know sweat. They know work. They know nothing ever came easy, nor will it ever come easy. They are hard . . . hard, I'm telling you."

It had been, as Carmody noted afterward, "an emotional week," which no doubt contributed to the letdown that produced a 13-6 loss to Louisiana Tech in the season finale. Moreover, the victory in Tuscaloosa did not erase the probation, and distractions, including more trouble with the NCAA, continued to plague the program. In February 1985 USM found itself on probation for another two years, the second of which the NCAA suspended along with all sanctions because of "the prompt disciplinary action taken by the university." That action had included two controversial firings of assistant coaches, one of whom later won a substantial judgment against the school in a state

court. His suit and another for breach of contract by an applicant for an assistant coaching job kept Carmody, Dale, and Lucas in and out of courtrooms frequently during the 1980s.

In 1986 a beleagured Dale announced his retirement. He had seen the best of times and the worst of times, but under his direction USM had established itself as an institution of prominence in college athletics. Perhaps his finest achievement was the school's entrance into the prestigious Metro athletic conference in June 1982. Lucas underscored Dale's accomplishments when he noted that "our ascendency in athletics has been very beneficial in terms of attracting students, and it has been particularly helpful in focusing the attention of people all over the country on this university, which was really not known outside the Southeast."

Ironically, the man chosen to replace Dale, Terry Don Phillips of Southwestern Louisiana, accepted the post only to change his mind, as Dale himself had done when USM first offered him its head coaching position in 1969. Southern then turned to former Clemson athletic director Bill McLellan, who in 1986 became only the third director of athletics in USM history.

Ace Cleveland became Southern's sports information director in 1957 and served for almost three decades. At his retirement in 1986, the university named the M. M. Roberts Stadium press box in his honor.

Despite all the upheaval, Carmody's team continued to prosper on the football field. Impressive wins over Ole Miss (27-7) and Mississippi State (31-6)—the seventh in a row against the Bulldogs—highlighted a 7-4 season in 1983, during which Louis Lipps became the second leading pass receiver in school history. He went on to become the Pittsburgh Steelers' top draft choice and NFL Rookie of the Year in 1984. The Eagles opened 1984 between the hedges in Georgia's storied Sanford Stadium, where Rex Banks kicked a school record four field goals to match the effort of Bulldog Kevin Butler and help set an NCAA record for the most combined field goals in a single game. Southern's bid for an upset fell short 26-19 and launched a disappointing injury-plagued year that ended 4-7, Carmody's only losing season at the Southern helm. His squad rebounded in 1985 to give him his third 7-4 record since taking over the program, and the following year's team notched the school's seventh winning campaign in eight seasons. The highlight of 1986 came against Mississippi State. Leading 24-21 with barely four minutes to play, the Bulldogs punted the ball dead at the Eagle two yard line. But in an incredible drive that symbolized the football program's steady march for-

ward since 1976, USM's offense drove 98 yards to a thrilling 28-24 victory.

Carmody's 31-24 record over five seasons gave him the best start of any Southern coach since Pie Vann and left the school's mark at 144-106-5 since becoming a major institution, a winning percentage of 57.6 that ranks among the best in college football.

Golden Eagle basketball also blossomed in the 1980s. The 1980–81 team, led by freshman playmaker Curtis Green and junior forward Joe Dawson, finished 20-7 and gained the school's first berth in the National Invitational Tournament. Perhaps the turning point came in January 1981, when Turk took his team to Milwaukee where an 84-72 upset of perennial midwestern power Marquette earned the Eagles national recognition. Other big wins came over Oklahoma, Mississippi State, and Memphis State, but a capacity crowd at Reed Green Coliseum saw the season end with a disappointing two-point loss to Holy Cross in the opening round of the NIT. After a 15-11 finish the next year, USM encountered a major challenge in 1982–83 with its first season in the Metro Conference, whose premier team, the University of Louisville, had captured the national championship only

three years earlier. The Eagles struggled at the beginning, winning only ten conference games in its first three seasons in the league. After a 14-14 mark in 1982–83 and 13-15 the following year, Southern sank to a dismal 7-21 in 1984–85. But the play of several freshmen and a big home win over Louisville nurtured hopes of a better future. Things turned around dramatically in 1985–86. After heartbreaking near misses at home against top-ranked Memphis State and eventual national champion Louisville, USM won eight of its last ten regular season games. The fourth place finish in the conference and 17-10 record overall was enough to win Metro Coach of the Year for Turk and a second trip to the NIT for the team. But postseason wins remained elusive for the Eagles, who dropped a one-point game to Cincinnati in the conference tournament and an 81-71 decision to Florida in the NIT.

With five returning starters and three outstanding transfers, Turk's troops began 1986–87 with high hopes. Despite an impressive win over North Texas State in the school's first appearance on national television, Southern struggled to a 9-2 start and then limped to a disappointing 17-11 regular season finish. A single victory over Virginia Tech in

By 1985 USM offered intramural competition for men and women in more than forty sports. Portland McCaskill, opposite page, finished her career in 1985 as the most prolific scorer and rebounder in the history of women's basketball at USM.

the Metro tournament, the school's first since joining the league, eased the pain somewhat and earned USM its third NIT bid since 1980. Whatever indifference the lackluster season might have bred toward postseason play dissolved into unbridled exuberance when the tournament committee announced that Southern would host a first round game against the University of Mississippi. Fans stood in line for hours as tickets to basketball in Reed Green Coliseum finally became what M. K. Turk had long hoped to make them, a precious commodity. And the growing excitement rejuvenated his players who gave the boisterous capacity crowd everything they could have hoped for, building a commanding 36-point lead before cruising to a 93-75 win. The USM community was stunned when the tournament committee passed over Hattiesburg as a second round site and sent the Eagles to play St. Louis University in Kiel Auditorium. The team responded with an 83-78 overtime win, but for the second time the committee shunned Green Coliseum scheduling Southern's third round battle with Vanderbilt in Nashville. Again, however, the Eagles responded with a win, 95-88, despite squandering an 18-point first half lead.

All of Mississippi's attention seemed focused on New York as Turk took his team to Madison Square Garden for a semifinal match with Big Eight power Nebraska. Sophomores Jurado Hinton and Randy Pettus came off the bench to spark a sputtering offense and overcome an early 13-point Cornhusker lead. The 82-75 win put USM in the finals against a powerful LaSalle team. Several hundred fans followed the team to New York, while thousands of alumni and friends throughout the state and the nation watched on cable television as John White made a crucial steal with but six seconds to play and then calmly dropped two free throws through the net to seal an 84-80 victory and give USM the first national basketball tournament championship ever won by a men's team from Mississippi. "There are just rewards for hard work," Turk told a postgame press conference, "and this is an example." Junior point guard Casey Fisher put it more bluntly: "They gave us the hardest road, but now there's nothing they can do about it." The victory was particularly sweet for lone senior Kenny Siler to whom the disappointing regular season must have seemed especially bitter.

Kay James's Lady Eagles also distinguished themselves in the 1980s, appearing in the AIAW tournament (1981), the Women's NIT (1982), and the NCAA tournament (1985 and 1987). The 1984–85 squad hosted the Metro tournament after finishing the regular season at 19-7 to give James her eighth consecutive winning season. Portland McCaskill, the most prolific scorer and rebounder in Lady Eagle history, led USM past Louisville and South Carolina to earn a spot in the finals against powerful Memphis State. In one of the most exciting athletic contests ever played on the USM campus, the Tigers edged James's squad 77-75 in overtime. Two years later Southern again made it to the Metro finals, this time against South Carolina. Tournament MVP Lesha Franklin led the Lady Eagles to a 68-66 win that gave USM its first Metro championship in any sport. Nineteen eighty-seven was truly a championship year for Golden Eagle basketball.

The overall athletic program expanded steadily under Roland Dale in the eighties. In 1984 the baseball team, under new coach Hill Denson, occupied a new facility named for retired coach Pete Taylor. By 1987 USM participated in 14 varsity

sports, 8 for men (football, basketball, baseball, tennis, golf, indoor and outdoor track, and cross country) and 6 for women (basketball, tennis, volleyball, softball, track, and cross country).

After three quarters of a century, student life had become rich and varied. Three new fraternities (Sigma Chi, 1981; Phi Beta Sigma, 1982; and Delta Tau Delta, 1984) had appeared, and there were more than 200 active student organizations on campus. An intramural athletic program offered competition in forty sports ranging from football and basketball to water polo and frisbee. Almost seventy percent of all students shared a total of more than $12 million in various kinds of financial aid; 2300 students held part-time campus employment, a total annual payroll of almost $3 million. The Commons, which was completely renovated in 1982, hired a registered dietician and added a self-service soup and salad bar and a self-service drink fountain. An active Associated Student Body offered a variety of student government services and events, and the University Activities Council sponsored top name entertainment. In addition, gallery showings, recitals, plays, and musical and dance concerts provided a wide range of cultural activities.

Southern to the Top

The accomplishments of the 1987 NIT champions seemed endless. Randolph Keys, opposite page, garnered the Tournament's Most Valuable Player award, and Derrick Hamilton joined him on the all-NIT team. Keys, Casey Fisher, left, and Kenny Siler, with trophy, all entered USM's 1000-point club, and Fisher set a school record for career assists. Even the radio voice of the Eagles, John Cox, a product of USM's department of radio, television, and film, received Mississippi's Sportscaster of the Year award from the National Sportscaster and Sportswriter Association. The 23 wins was the most by a USM team in a quarter of a century and gave Coach M. K. Turk a career record of 163–143. It was a memorable and fitting way to celebrate 75 years of basketball that began on an outdoor dirt court behind Forrest County Hall. In his 1954 tribute to Lee Floyd, Jimmie McDowell had predicted that one day Southern would "become a big-time ball club—a team that may eventually play in Madison Square Garden." Twenty three years later, that prediction came true in spectacular fashion. It was team barber and unofficial spokesman Casey Fisher who best described what the scrappy underdogs from a former teachers college in south Mississippi had done: "We came, we saw, and we tore the house down."

"In the final analysis," Alma Hickman had once said, "education involves students, teachers, and books." By the 1980s those aspects of USM's life had progressed on a scale grander than "Miss Alma" could have imagined even three decades before when she had stated that conviction, and certainly in 1912 when she had witnessed those elements of the institution in their infancy. The student body of 227 homesick souls whom Willard Bond had faced in 1912 had grown to more than 13,000 by 1982, and not only were there more students, there were better students. In the decade after 1974, the average ACT score of incoming students rose from 19.2 to 19.8; those with scores above 27 increased from 63 to 102, while those below 15 declined from 95 to 69. The 1985–86 academic year began with a reorganized and revitalized Honors College under Dean Peggy Prennshaw. To sustain these advances in the quality of its students, USM adopted stiffer admission and academic progress requirements, along with a new program of academic advisement. In response to a national reemphasis on general education, the university in 1985 instituted an expanded core curriculum that included composition (6 hours), algebra or higher mathematics (3), fine arts (3), world liter-ature (3), world history (6), social and behavioral sciences (6), natural and applied sciences (11), human wellness (2), and electives (6).

The president's conviction that teachers are the heart and soul of a university continued to bear rich fruit. The faculty of seventeen that Joe Cook had assembled in 1912 had become almost six hundred by 1986, sixty-five percent of them with terminal degrees and ninety-eight percent with at least a master's degree. Lucas had also emphasized the responsibility to nurture and reward professors, and he pursued those goals vigorously. But the fight for adequate funds remained, as Alma Hickman had described it from the beginning, the institution's "hardest battle." Salaries, research funds, and support services all remained well below national standards and at times demoralized the faculty. As the Southern Association committee noted after its reaccreditation visit in 1985, "At a time when the institution seems poised for a giant step forward the financial resources available to the state are on the decline." Nonetheless, by 1985 Lucas could take pride in having achieved one of his early promises, to make USM professors the highest paid in Mississippi. With a vice president specifically designated to supervise and support faculty research, the university appointed a director of research and sponsored programs with expertise in funded research and patent applications. During the first half of the eighties alone, USM faculty received almost $20 million in grants for research, and in 1986 the figure reached an unprecedented $6.3 million.

At the same time, the administration expected significant achievement from its faculty. In 1985 Lucas approved a new university policy on tenure and promotion that set standards of excellence for faculty who sought higher rank and continued employment. In the words of the 1983 institutional self-study, "The University now places a growing emphasis on the professional distinction of its faculty; personnel decisions are now directly linked to scholarly and artistic achievement. Competence in the classroom remains important and faculty are also expected to perform a wide range of other institutional and community service, but scholarly, creative, and professional endeavors are valued as never before."

Southern's faculty responded admirably to the challenge. Nineteen eighty-five proved to be the most fruitful of a succession of productive years, as USM professors contributed 60 books, 439 articles,

925 artistic performances, 610 professional papers, 7 sound recordings, and 4 patents to the world of scholarship. The Southern Association committee declared that "faculty at the University of Southern Mississippi are professionally active and should be commended . . . Many departments are quite productive." Examples of that productivity illustrate that at its best, the work of Southern's professors compared favorably with that of their counterparts at America's finest institutions:

The work of a member of the music department premiered in April 1983, at the John F. Kennedy Center in Washington, D.C. The same professor was selected to write the score for the soundtrack of Mississippi ETV's "Passover," narrated by television star Ed Asner. In 1982 *Musical America* named as its "Young Artist of the Year" another USM professor of music who three years later presented a recital at Carnegie Hall. A third member of the music faculty was selected in 1981 to perform the leading role in the National Touring Company of the New York City Opera's production of *La Traviata*.

The dean of the School of Nursing became only the second Mississippian admitted as a Fellow of the Academy of American Nurses.

The chairman of foreign languages spent 1982–83 as Fulbright professor of comparative literature at the University of Alexandria in Egypt.

Several members of the English department won international literary prizes for fiction and poetry, and the director of USM's Center for Writers published several short stories in the *New Yorker* magazine and also received critical acclaim for his novels in such publications as *Time*, *Newsweek*, and the *New York Times Book Review*. An advisory board of distinguished literary scholars chose another English professor to edit the Variorum Edition of the works of poet John Donne. Another, who edited three definitive editions of William Faulkner's novels for Random House publishers, was one of a handful of American scholars invited to deliver one of the plenary lectures at a 1983 Moscow Conference on the famous Mississippi novelist.

The director of USM's School of Communications was chosen to edit *The Olympic Record*, official daily newspaper of the 1984 Los Angeles Olympics.

A computer science professor won the world computer chess championship and was invited to address American scientists at the Los Alamos Scientific Laboratory and to attend the International Conference on Man-Machine Interaction in Paris.

The chairman of sociology served as Mississippi's delegate to a White House Conference on Aging in 1981.

A professor of engineering technology received the American Society for Engineering Education Award for 1983.

The U.S. Department of Defense chose a USM professor as an official historian for the celebration of the 40th anniversary of the Allied invasion of Normandy (D-Day). Another member of the history department received a coveted MacArthur Fellowship which paid his salary and research expenses for five years. A third won an award from the Organization of American Historians for the best first book by an American historian in 1986.

A USM political science professor served as international affairs editor for *USA Today*.

In 1984 a member of the psychology department earned a prestigious Young Researcher of the Year Award of over $100,000 from the National Institutes of Health to support his research.

A polymer science professor was one of seven U.S. scientists invited to present lectures to the second U.S.–Romanian Seminar in New and Modified Polymers, and another was chosen to deliver the Mattiello Lecture to the Federation of Societies for Coatings Technology. A third ap-

peared on the cover of a Yugoslavian science journal which featured his research.

Again this emphasis on research and scholarship did not come at the expense of classroom instruction. The committee of the Southern Association commended the university for the quality of its teaching and heaped special praise on several schools:

> The quality and effectiveness of instruction is clearly the strength of the School [of health, physical education, and recreation].
>
> Faculty members [in home economics] are going beyond normal duties to teach their students and serve the community.
>
> Effective instruction seems to be a matter of pride among Liberal Arts faculty and student opinions seem to support this view.

The library, as it had been since Anna Roberts's day, continued to be one of the areas where lack of funds pressed the university hardest. The 1973 self-study had set a target of 1.5 million volumes for the library which would have tripled its holdings. Though the university did not reach that goal by 1983, it made significant progress. The combined libraries contained almost a million volumes by 1985, and expenditure for acquisitions had al-

most doubled since 1977. Consultants for undergraduate program reviews found library resources adequate, but problems remained for some graduate programs. The McCain Graduate Library and Archives held several valuable special collections including the Sam Woods Collection of rare books and artifacts; the Lena Y. de Grummond Collection of children's literature; an excellent genealogy collection; the Earnest A. Walen Civil War collection; records of the Association of American Railroads

and the Gulf, Mobile, and Ohio Railroad Company; and the extensive papers of two of Mississippi's leading twentieth century political figures, Theodore G. Bilbo and William M. Colmer. The library's Teaching-Learning Resource Center established a reputation for excellence and creativity that earned it the 1981 G. Theodore Mittau Award of the American Association of State Colleges and Universities for innovation and change in public education.

A Scholar's Legacy

USM's English department owns an interesting heritage. Mississippi Normal College's first English chairman, Joseph McMillin, retired in 1926 to Louisville in Winston County. There he took under his intellectual wing a strapping young country boy from nearby Boon named Thomas Daniel Young. McMillin, Young later recalled, "was the first man I knew who had books of poetry and novels," and the old scholar introduced the younger one to Tennyson, Matthew Arnold, Dickens, and King Arthur's Knights of the Round Table. Armed with this "high-level personal tutoring," Young went on to study English at State Teachers College after which he earned a Ph.D. from Vanderbilt University. He returned to Mississippi Southern College in 1950 where he was himself chairman of the English department until 1957. He later went back to Vanderbilt and became English chairman there from 1967 to 1972. While teaching at Vanderbilt he took under his wing a graduate student, Tom Richardson, who was from Mrs. Young's home community of Rose Hill, Mississippi, and a 1962 graduate of USM. After earning a Ph.D. under Young at Vanderbilt, Richardson returned to USM where in 1984 he became, almost by right of inheritance, chairman of the English department.

enrolled is significantly moving the institution toward its goal of becoming a distinguished university. Strong administrative and academic leadership and a positive campus morale were visible to the committee. The framework for becoming a comprehensive distinguished university is clearly present."

And indeed Southern's growth and progress had been remarkable. Since the first degree class in 1922, it had awarded almost 65,000 degrees, more than half of them after 1972. It listed 5250 available courses in fifty-three departments and ninety-three fields; it offered eighteen different graduate degrees through 102 programs. It was affiliated with the publication of ten scholarly journals. Its Honors College was one of only fourteen in the United States. USM was the first institution in Mississippi with accredited undergraduate, graduate, and continuing education programs in nursing and the first in the nation to offer bachelor's, master's, and doctoral degrees in polymer science. It was one of only fifteen institutions in the nation to offer three fully accredited doctoral programs in psychology, one of only four to hold accreditation in all four fine arts disciplines—art, dance, theatre, and music. Southern's English department had been

The USM graduate school also prospered with enrollment increasing thirty percent between 1972 and 1983. Nonetheless, the staff of the state college board recommended elimination of several doctoral programs in 1986. The board rejected the staff recommendation, recognizing, as the Southern Association committee had put it, that USM "has a number of extremely strong graduate programs taught by talented, productive faculty. They deserve defense against unwarranted decisions by the Board to downgrade or terminate them. Rather than duplicate programs offered elsewhere in the state, these are healthy alternatives which need and deserve greater support inside and outside the University."

USM received full reaccreditation from the Southern Association in 1985. The agency's report in summary acknowledged that "today the University is the largest . . . in Mississippi serving more than 13,000. . . . Quality of faculty and students ranked in the top ten percent in the nation, its dean of home economics was elected president of the American Dietetics Association for 1988–89, and in 1987 a member of its science faculty served as president of the largest professional organization in the world, the American Chemical Society. In 1984 USM's president was elected to head the 354 member American Association of State Colleges and Universities.

Aubrey Lucas began his presidency in 1975 with a significant address in which he set before the university community the goal of becoming a distinguished university. After a decade of progress toward that goal, he delivered another important address in 1986 to the Newcomen Society of Mississippi, which chose to honor USM on its seventy-fifth anniversary. Speaking this time to leaders of Mississippi's business and industrial community, Lucas recalled his earlier speech and its theme of excellence, and he sketched USM's progress in pursuit of academic distinction. "It is appropriate, however," he suggested, "for us to redefine what we mean by excellence. Traditionally, we have judged excellence by the standards of . . . Harvard, Yale, Stanford, and Berkeley. These institu-

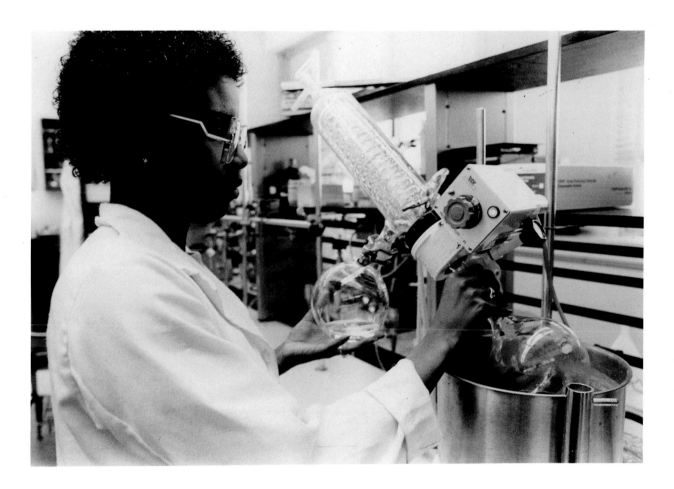

tions represent what is generally considered the best in American higher education, and it is good that we emulate their dedication to the creation, preservation, and dissemination of knowledge. But we make a mistake if we believe that excellence comes only when we achieve a reputation that rivals Harvard's. We condemn ourselves to repeated failure if we establish this as our course. Instead, we must acknowledge that in Mississippi there is a different path toward distinction. Our goal must be to develop the human capital of this state. We will achieve excellence only to the extent that we have programs of study and centers of activity that change our people for the better."

The president stressed that USM must not abandon the quest for academic distinction toward which it had made so much progress. "We will continue to do," he insisted, "what we have always done—and done well . . . educate our students broadly, helping them . . . to live creatively and joyfully as well as acquire the skills . . . to establish a satisfying career, but this will not be sufficient to develop the human potential of this state. After all, many Mississippians do not seek nor do they need a collegiate education. What is our obligation to them . . . How can we in public education . . . help to remove the unwarranted stigma attached to so many good and deserving Mississippians simply because our state ranks at the bottom in many social, economic, and educational indices?"

It was the same question that young Orville Brim had asked himself on that foggy, frigid morning almost three quarters of a century before. Across the stump-scarred ruggedness, through the cold mist, he had watched Mississippi's human potential parade slowly before him in the bed of a horse-drawn wagon. And he was moved, not by anger or contempt or even pity, but by respect, respect for a simple but noble people most of whom, through no fault of their own, carried "an unwarranted stigma" simply because they ranked at the bottom of certain socio-economic indices. He was also moved by faith, by the firm conviction that the little normal college whose faculty he had recently joined could not so much change these people, as help create an environment in which they could freely change themselves. His respect for such people reminded him that the value of a better life was inseparable from the development of human character involved in achieving it. It came to him in the form of an adage, one that would come back to

A Model of Excellence

USM's department of polymer science offers an inspiring model of the university's march toward academic distinction. The program evolved out of the Pan American Tung Research and Development League laboratory, below, which moved to the campus from Picayune in 1963. South Mississippi, along with Argentina, were the world's major producers of tung oil and USM worked hard to develop uses for the product. Ironically, polymer science, under the leadership of chairman Shelby Thames, became a separate department of USM in 1970 shortly after Hurricane Camille destroyed Pearl River County's tung trees. Over the next 15 years, the department became one of the country's two leading polymer science research institutions and one of only four offering both undergraduate and graduate degrees in the field. During that time the university awarded 150 bachelor's, 50 master's, and 28 Ph.D. degrees (10 in 1985–86 alone) in polymer science. The program, which does research on projects ranging from plastics for artificial hearts to spacesuits to fuel conserving coatings for seagoing ship hulls, emphasizes industrial experience in order to acquaint students with the demands of the work force. With its graduates in great demand, the department attracts a substantial amount of industrial scholarship money each year in addition to research grants, which totaled $1.6 million in 1985–86 alone. The Critical Agricultural Material Act, which passed Congress in November 1986, allocated a $10 million grant to USM for construction of a two-story polymer science research facility, which could prove to be a major contribution to Mississippi's economic development by luring polymer-related industries to the state. The university's polymer science program epitomizes USM's vision of being a distinguished university, making significant contributions to the development of human capital in the state and region.

Professor Shelby Thames with artificial heart made from polymers. USM announces $10 million federal grant to build polymer science facility. From left are U.S. Senator Thad Cochran, President Lucas, Professor Shelby Thames, and polymer science chairman Gordon Nelson. In October 1986, Professor Nelson was elected president of the American Chemical Society, the world's largest professional scientific organization.

him fifty years later as he reflected upon the determination and sacrifice of that first generation of normal college students, most of whom themselves sprang from the kind of people he had seen on that wagon.

Here, perhaps, lies Southern's—and Mississippi's—different path to distinction. When one thinks of Harvard, one thinks of brilliance—which by no means implies that a university that produced Thomas Daniel Young or a state that produced William Faulkner lacks brilliance. When one thinks of the University of Southern Mississippi, perhaps one ought to think of perseverance—which by no means implies that a university founded by New England Puritans lacks a laboring spirit. It is simply a matter of perception. As USM's 1983 self-study noted, "changes in how the University perceives itself" are important. One of the issues raised by the nature of USM's recent development is "student and faculty involvement in the changing definition of the University's self-image and their satisfaction with its priorities." Men like Orville Brim and Joe Cook left little room for doubt regarding their sense of satisfaction with the institution's self-image. They established for that institution a rich heritage, one symbolized by

NBC correspondent and USM alumnus Chuck Scarborough, right, addresses graduates at 1987 commencement ceremonies.

Brim's phrase "dearly bought, deeply treasured." Rather than bemoan the economic, social, and educational status of their institution and its constituents, these men set before themselves the task of making that status better, and they gloried in the struggle with neither shame nor apology. Those who came after them have sustained that struggle for seventy-five years, and USM's current generation cannot ignore this heritage.

In many ways, M. K. Turk's NIT victors symbolize the renewal of that legacy. Accepting the challenge of a basketball program that almost everyone told him was ranked at the bottom and would forever remain there, Turk took players from places like Utica and Waynesboro, Collins and Richton, and made them champions. They were not so much extraordinary athletes, but ordinary athletes who achieved extraordinary things, through hard work, discipline, and devotion to each other and to the university.

Perhaps an even better example is another athlete, a young black football player, who came to Southern as an insecure and inarticulate freshman and became an outstanding defensive lineman. More important, however, he enrolled in USM's school of communication and worked as hard in

the classroom as he did on the practice field. He never earned the coveted opportunity to play professional football, but he earned a degree, and embarked on a bright future in broadcast journalism. "I never thought I'd be in a position where I would be able to speak freely," he recalled, "have confidence in my speaking, but Southern has been a great school for me, and if I had to tell anybody where to go to school, they need to come to the Hub City." His success is a tribute to so many—like Joe Cook and Orville Brim, Anna Roberts, J. Fred Walker, R. A. McLemore, and William D. McCain—who labored so faithfully to give USM its heritage of distinction.

"It has been well said," Aubrey Lucas noted at the outset of the university's Diamond Jubilee, "that where there is no vision, the people perish. We at the University of Southern Mississippi have a vision, a vision which requires us to stretch our imaginations, to use our resources very wisely and to work harder, perhaps, than might otherwise be required. This vision has brought us, over these seventy-five years, from significant but really rather humble beginnings, to a university whose programs and whose people are becoming truly distinguished."